PRAISE FOR

Mark Di Vincenzo and His Previous Book,
BUY KETCHUP IN MAY AND FLY AT NOON

"The breezy little paperback offers hundreds of tips from the former investigative reporter, whose research is evident and sources carefully listed at the end. That keeps the attribution from cluttering up the info, which ranges from sublime to silly."
—*Los Angeles Times* travel blog

"Well worth checking out." —*Dayton Daily News*

"Food for thought." —*Boston Globe*

"Sure to liven up a boring cocktail party . . . [W]ill enlighten, surprise, even disappoint you." —*Houston Chronicle*

"Straightforward." —*Richmond Times-Dispatch*

"Full of amusing and helpful timing tips." —*Sacramento Bee*

"Strangely compelling." —*Guardian* (UK)

"[Di Vincenzo] doles out advice with practical reasoning . . . [U]seful and interesting." —*Cleveland Plain Dealer*

"[Di Vincenzo] gets into the nitty-gritty of why timing really is everything."
—*Chicago Tribune*

© Amy Jackson

ABOUT THE AUTHOR

As a journalist with nearly a quarter century of experience, MARK DI VINCENZO made a name for himself as a reporter who exposed abuses and as a writer who made the complicated seem simple. He won numerous awards before becoming an editor.

During the summer of 2007, he left daily journalism to pursue book projects and to start Business Writers Group, a writing and public relations company. In 2009, Harper-Collins published his first book, *Buy Ketchup in May and Fly At Noon: A Guide to the Best Time to Buy This, Do That and Go There,* a *New York Times* bestseller. (www.buyketchup inmay.com)

Born and reared in Cleveland, he lives in the shipyard town of Newport News, Virginia—two blocks from William Styron's childhood home—with his wife and two daughters. A third daughter attends the University of Oklahoma.

ALSO BY
MARK DI VINCENZO

Buy Ketchup in May and Fly at Noon:
A Guide to the Best Time to Buy This, Do That and Go There

YOUR PINKIE IS MORE POWERFUL THAN YOUR THUMB

And 333 Other Surprising Facts That Will
Make You Wealthier, Healthier and Smarter
than Everyone Else

MARK DI VINCENZO

HARPER

NEW YORK • LONDON • TORONTO • SYDNEY

HARPER

Designed by Justin Dodd

ISBN 978-0-06-200835-0

FOR
ANGELA,
OLIVIA
&
SOPHIA

CONTENTS

ACKNOWLEDGMENTS

Thanks to Kate Nintzel, my wordsmith; to Michelle Wolfson, my advocate; and to Jayne Di Vincenzo, my best friend.

INTRODUCTION

As far back as I can remember, I've found the truth stranger—and more interesting—than fiction. Even as a boy, I avoided comic books and Hardy Boys mysteries and devoured newspapers and magazines, often sharing what I discovered with others. It came as no surprise to my family and friends that I pursued journalism, an adventure in which I was actually paid, though never very well, to play the role of the messenger. After twenty-four years as a newspaperman—seventeen as a reporter and seven as an editor—I quit to start a writing and editing company, but the bug to tell others about the fascinating and surprising nuggets I discovered never left me.

In recent years, the recipient of much of this information has been my wife, who shares my enthusiasm for the oddities sometimes found within current events. It was my wife who came up with the idea for my first book, *Buy Ketchup in May and Fly at Noon:*

A Guide to the Best Time to Buy This, Do That and Go There. The confidence I gained from writing *Buy Ketchup* convinced me I could write another book, a compilation of the freshest, most interesting, and most surprising information I came across. What I ended up with is *Your Pinkie Is More Powerful Than Your Thumb,* a quirky fact book like no other.

Your Pinkie Is More Powerful Than Your Thumb focuses on the most recent discoveries in health, science, history, and more. This is not a book where you'll find out who can eat the most hotdogs, who's covered with the most tattoos, or who weighs the most.

Your Pinkie Is More Powerful Than Your Thumb is a book in which you'll find the answers to questions you'd never think to ask:

How did Hitler act at the dinner table?

What's the happiest job in science?

What can you expect to get in a trade for a woolly mammoth?

Which beverage is more environmentally friendly—beer, tea, coffee, wine, or milk?

What's more—3 dollars or 300 cents?

Where is the most dangerous place in the world to be an albino?

What percentage of doctors in China smoke?

But *Your Pinkie Is More Powerful Than Your Thumb* is more than just a compilation of facts. It's loaded with dozens and dozens of money- and health-related tips that can help make you healthier and wealthier. And smarter.

Although I can't promise you that reading this book will cause you to live longer and get richer, I can promise that you'll learn a lot and be better off for it.

ONE

LETTING IT ALL HANG OUT IN NAURU

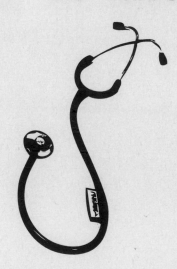

W here—or what's—Nauru? Keep reading. You're about to learn a lot about recent health-related discoveries your doctor probably doesn't even know about. You'll learn about whether you should bother with multivitamins, how much hair you lose every day, why it turns gray, and why you should care a lot if you can't touch your toes. Speaking of your digits, you'll learn about why life without your pinkie fingers would make you miserable and which nation is most visionary when it comes to kidney transplants. (You won't believe it.)

WHY ARE HOSPITALS SO WORRIED ABOUT NECKTIES?

Neckties, regardless of who wears them, are rarely cleaned, and doctors' ties, which are more likely to be bombarded with bacteria from sneezes and coughs, can unknowingly spread disease to patients. The British Medical Association recommends doctors avoid wearing neckties and other "functionless" clothes that can serve "as superbugs." The American Medical Association may consider a similar resolution after it compiles more scientific evidence. Those who want doctors to shed their neckties point to a 2004 study of ties worn by employees of New York Hospital Medical Center of Queens in which half of the doctors' ties contained germs that could cause illnesses. Only 10 percent of the neckties worn by hospital security guards carried similar germs. **What you can do:** This research, doctors say, just goes to show the importance of washing not only our hands—and bodies—but also our clothing, furniture, and carpeting.

HOW MANY DIFFERENT SPECIES OF BACTERIA ARE ON YOUR HANDS RIGHT NOW, AND WHY ARE LAW ENFORCEMENT OFFICIALS EXCITED ABOUT THAT?

About 150. And about 135 of those are fairly unique to each person. Forensic experts and other law enforcement professionals predict that one day they'll be able to use bacteria to prove who touched an object, even if a criminal wiped away his fingerprints. Researchers compared bacteria on a computer mouse with bacteria from the computer user and 270 other randomly chosen people and found that the closest match was to the person who used the mouse. The researchers expect that the technique they used will improve, leading to better accuracy. Right now their findings are correct between 70 percent and 90 percent of the time. **What you can do:** Washing your hands is a good way to kill germs and stop the spread of disease. Spend at least twenty seconds washing your hands. Despite what your mother always told you about using hot water, researchers have found that water temperature has no effect on soap's ability to kill germs. Studies show washing hands with soap can kill diarrheal disease by 45 percent.

IF YOU'RE TRYING TO CHOOSE JUST THE RIGHT DOCTOR, WHAT'S ONE OF THE MOST IMPORTANT THINGS YOU NEED TO FIND OUT?

If your doctor sees you at the grocery store or at the library, will he approach you and say hi or hide behind a shelf? In other words, is he an extrovert? A new study suggests that medical schools would do everyone a big favor if they required would-be doctors to take a personality test as well as the Medical College Admission Test, or MCAT, the standardized test that measures mastery of premed courses. Three psychologists gave more than 600 Belgian medical students a standardized personality test that focused on extraversion, neuroticism, openness, agreeableness, and conscientiousness. The researchers kept in touch with the students for nearly a decade and concluded that extroverts often struggled early on in medical school but usually excelled as they spent less time in the classroom and more time with patients. While conscientious students also did well throughout medical school, extroversion was the most telling sign that students would succeed. Bad news if you're sensitive: Students who were more likely to become emotionally upset struggled in school. **Bonus question: Which prestigious medical school accepts students who don't take organic chemistry, physics, or the MCAT?** Mount Sinai School of Medicine, in New York City. The school reserves slots for about thirty-five students a year who don't take the traditional premedical school curriculum and maintain a 3.5 grade point average as an undergraduate.

BAD BOSSES CAN BE A PAIN IN THE YOU-KNOW-WHAT. WHERE ELSE CAN THEY BE A PAIN?

In the heart. Swedish researchers found that men who had to endure incompetent and inconsiderate supervisors were more likely to suffer from heart disease. The researchers tracked 3,100 men between the ages of nineteen and seventy, checking their hearts at work between 1992 and 1995. By 2003, seventy-four had suffered from heart attacks, angina, or some other sort of heart disease. Those with bad bosses were 60 percent more likely than those with good bosses to suffer heart disease, and the longer the men worked for a bad boss, the more likely they were to have heart problems. In fact, having a bad boss in this study was a more accurate predictor of heart disease than an employee's smoking or exercise habits, weight or cholesterol. **What you can do:** A bad boss is the top reason why people quit their jobs. If you don't want to leave your company: (1) talk with your boss and be direct and professional, (2) get advice from the human resources department, and (3) ask for a transfer to another department.

COUNTING SHEEP IS SO BORING THAT IT'S BOUND TO PUT YOU TO SLEEP, RIGHT?

Wrong. It's actually *too* boring. Researchers split insomniacs into three groups and told one group to visualize a relaxing scene—a babbling brook, for example—and told the second group to distract themselves by counting sheep. A third group was given no instructions at all. Insomniacs who were told to visualize a relaxing scene fell asleep twenty minutes sooner than those who were not given those instructions. The researchers theorize that the relaxing scenes take up "cognitive space" in the insomniacs' brains and keep them from thinking about the worries or concerns that keep them from falling asleep. As for counting sheep, the researchers conclude it's so monotonous that few people can do it for very long, and so it's not very effective. **What you can do:** Think of that babbling brook or crashing waves or falling rain or whatever you find relaxing.

WHY IS IT SO IMPORTANT TO BE FIT IN YOUR FIFTIES?

Because if you're fit in your fifties, you double your chances of living to eighty-five. And if you're not fit then, you reduce your lifespan by an average of eight years. Those are the conclusions from a recently published study that tracked 1,444 men and 321 women in their fifties. The research began in the 1970s, when doctors began performing physical exams on fifty-somethings. By 2006, 906 men and 238 women of the original group were still alive and at least eighty-five years old. The researchers found that men were 1.8 times more likely to make it to eighty-five if they were fit in their fifites and women were 2.2 times more likely. **What you can do:** Doctors advise middle-aged people to participate in at least moderate exercise—brisk walking, doubles tennis, or ballroom dancing, for example—thirty minutes a day, five days a week. Already doing that? A new study that followed 34,079 healthy women recommends that women exercise sixty minutes a day to keep from gaining weight as they age.

IF YOU'RE IN YOUR EARLY SIXTIES, WHAT ARE THE ODDS THAT YOU'LL NEED NURSING HOME CARE AT SOME POINT DURING YOUR LIFE?

Four out of ten of you will require nursing home care. And it doesn't come cheap. In 2009, a private room at a nursing home cost an average of $219 a day in the United States, ranging from $584 a day in Alaska to $132 in Louisiana. **Want to stay at home?** You'll pay a home health aide an average of $21 an hour—as much as $30 an hour in Rochester, Minnesota, and as little as $13 an hour in Shreveport, Louisiana. **What you can do:** Short of moving to Louisiana, insurance agents and financial advisors advise people who don't want to live in a nursing home to buy home health care insurance, which has the potential to save you many thousands of dollars.

HOW MUCH HAIR DO WE LOSE EVERY DAY?

Fifty to one hundred strands. The good news is we usually grow that many replacement strands per day if we're physically and emotionally fit. But stress and a host of other health issues can cause us to lose more than we grow. Medicines that treat depression and acne or boost testosterone can lead to hair loss, and women also lose hair during menopause. Sometimes bad genes supersede everything else. In the United

States, about 50 million men and 30 million women lose hair because heredity isn't on their sides. **What you can do:** Americans spend about $180 million a year on hair-loss products, but dermatologists and other doctors warn that few products are effective. See a dermatologist who specializes in hair loss and ask for a scalp biopsy. The biopsy may hold clues to your hair loss. If it's due to iron deficiency, for example, take iron supplements.

THERE'S A GLOBAL SHORTAGE OF KIDNEYS FOR TRANSPLANTS, AND ONLY ONE COUNTRY HAS ENOUGH FOR THOSE WHO NEED THEM. WHICH IS IT?

Iran, which pays donors $1,200 and offers them free health insurance for one year. In addition, Iranian donors receive $2,300 to $4,500 from either the recipients or from charitable organizations. Iran has done this since 1988 and is believed to be the only nation without a shortage of kidneys for transplants. Singapore is considering paying organ donors as much as $50,000, and Israel has a program that makes it easier for people to receive organs if they are willing to donate them. In the United States in 2009, about 13,600 people received a kidney, about 3,500 people died while waiting for one, and more than 85,000 others were on waiting lists. Numerous economists, including a Nobel laureate, argue that there would be no shortage in the United States if donors were paid $15,000. Reports of black market sales indicate that kidneys go for about $20,000 in India, $40,000 in China, and $160,000 in Israel, with brokers making a tidy profit. **Bonus question #1: How much will you shorten your life if you donate a kidney?** Not at all, according to a study of all 80,347 people who donated a kidney between 1994 and 2009. Donors died no sooner on average than did members of a control group. **Bonus question #2: What other organs can you do without?** A lung, an eye, and some intestines, and, in rare cases, a pancreas. **What you can do:** As many as 120,000 Americans are on organ waiting lists of some kind. You can donate a kidney while you're alive, but it's obviously a lot less painful to donate your organs upon your death. You can sign up to do this when you receive or renew your driver's license.

JUST ABOUT ALL OF US HAVE HAD OUR HEARTS BROKEN, BUT CAN A HEART LITERALLY BREAK?
Yes. About 1 percent of heart attack sufferers had relatively clear, healthy arteries. In those cases, the heart attacks were caused by severe emotional or physical trauma that triggered a massive amount of adrenaline that overwhelms the heart and causes it to fail. Doctors have a name for what happens when emotional trauma triggers heart attacks: broken-heart syndrome. Here are five emotional traumas that have triggered heart attacks: losing a spouse, gambling away a lot of money, watching a pet suffer, getting lost in an unsafe neighborhood, and feeling overwhelmed by new computer software.

BY NOW MOST OF US KNOW THAT EATING A LOT OF FISH HELPS YOUR HEART STAY HEALTHY, BUT IS THERE ANY OTHER GOOD REASON TO EAT IT?
Yes. A study of about 15,000 seniors in nations as diverse as Chile, China, Cuba, the Dominican Republic, Mexico, Peru, India, and Venezuela found that people who ate fish almost every day were 20 percent less likely to suffer from dementia than those who ate it a few days a week. And those who ate it a few times a week were about 20 percent less likely to develop dementia than those who never ate it. **What you can do:** Can't afford to buy as much fish as you should eat? Doctors recommend taking fish oil supplements every day.

ATHEROSCLEROSIS, OR HARDENING OF THE ARTERIES, IS WIDELY BELIEVED TO BE A MODERN DISEASE, THE PRODUCT OF TOO MUCH FAST FOOD AND TOO LITTLE EXERCISE. TRUE?
False. A team of researchers—an Egyptian and four Americans—used CT scanning in 2009 to examine twenty-two especially well-preserved mummies at the Museum of Egyptian Antiquities in Cairo. They found a buildup of cholesterol in the arteries, a con-

dition that can lead to heart attacks and strokes. Of the twenty-two mummies, sixteen were members of Pharaoh Merneptah's court and lived somewhere between 1981 BC and 334 AD. Sixteen of the twenty-two were preserved well enough that the researchers could identify cardiovascular tissue, and of those sixteen, the researchers identified five confirmed cases of atherosclerosis and four probable cases. **What you can do:** The more we study cholesterol the more it seems to be a problem of genetics, but doctors say you can lower your cholesterol by eating healthier. Here's a list of some cholesterol-lowering foods found in just about every grocery store: oatmeal; oat bran; fatty fish such as salmon, trout, sardines, and fresh tuna; and walnuts, almonds, and other tree nuts.

MARIJUANA HAS BEEN PROVEN TO HELP RELIEVE PAIN AND CURB NAUSEA, AND IN RECENT YEARS, AN INCREASING NUMBER OF STATES HAVE LEGALIZED IT. BUT HOW ADDICTIVE IS IT COMPARED WITH OTHER DRUGS?

Nine percent of the people who tried it once became dependent, according to a study that included 8,098 people. The most addictive drug: tobacco (32 percent), followed by heroin (23 percent), cocaine (17 percent), alcohol (15 percent), stimulants other than cocaine (11 percent), sedatives and hypnotic drugs (9 percent), psychedelic drugs (5 percent), and inhalant drugs (4 percent). At least fourteen states have legalized marijuana for medicinal purposes, and others are considering it. Although marijuana can help with pain and nausea, it's not a cure-all: It also increases appetite and heart rate, causes drowsiness, and impairs memory and coordination. And for younger users, it's considered a gateway drug.

WOULD IT BE SUCH A BIG DEAL IF WE DIDN'T HAVE OUR PINKIE FINGERS?

A bigger deal than you might think. The pinkie finger and the ring finger give you power, and without the pinkie, you'd lose a whopping 50 percent of your hand strength. With reward comes risk: The pinkie, because it's on the end, is less protected than the other fingers and is fractured twice as often.

WHAT ABOUT YOUR TOES? IF YOU CAN'T TOUCH THEM, DOES THAT MEAN YOU'RE AN OUT-OF-SHAPE SLOB WHO'S GOING TO DIE BEFORE YOUR TIME?

Well, uh, maybe. According to a study of 526 healthy adults between twenty and eighty-three, those who couldn't touch their toes were more likely to have stiff arteries, which make it harder for the heart to move blood and can increase the risk for heart attacks and strokes. The researchers tested flexibility by having people sit on the floor with their legs straight and attempt to touch their toes. They tested their arterial flexibility by placing blood pressure cuffs on the ankles and arms of the participants. **Good news if you're younger:** The researchers saw a correlation between inflexible bodies and inflexible arteries in those over forty but not in those under forty. **What you can do:** Personal trainers say stretching is way underrated. Try stretching every day. Most bodies will react favorably to it and become more flexible the more you stretch.

MULTIVITAMINS HAVE A LITTLE OF EVERYTHING THAT OUR BODIES NEED, BUT CAN THEY BE COUNTED ON TO HELP PREVENT SERIOUS DISEASE, AS MANY PEOPLE BELIEVE?

Not really. An eight-year study of 161,808 postmenopausal women concluded that multivitamins did not lower the risk for a number of cancers or heart attacks, blood clots, and strokes. The researchers say it might make more sense to skip these vitamins and just make sure you eat a variety of healthy foods. Other studies on multivitamins have confirmed the results of this study while others said the supplements might help with some cancers. **What you can do:** Doctors agree that multivitamins help supplement our diets. Take them with meals because they absorb better into the body with food. **Bonus question: How about aspirin?** Doctors say it no longer makes sense to take an aspirin a day to reduce the risk of heart disease. In fact, aspirin may actually cause bleeding disorders and may do more harm than good for people not at risk for heart disease and stroke. **What you can do:** Consult your doctor, but a national health task force says a daily dose of aspirin is no longer recommended for men younger than forty-five, women younger than fifty-five, anyone older than eighty, and anyone with a history of ulcers.

CAN BLIND PEOPLE SEE ANYTHING WHEN THEY DREAM?

Mostly no. People who lose their vision before age five rarely see images when they dream. Those who lose their vision after age five see more, though less and less as they age.

HOW MANY TIMES A DAY DO AMERICANS SHOW UP IN A HOSPITAL EMERGENCY ROOM BECAUSE THEIR CAT OR DOG CAUSED THEM TO FALL?

About 237 times—or about 86,600 times a year. Nearly 88 percent of the injuries involved dogs, and nearly seven out of ten injuries involved girls or women. The actual number of pet-related injuries is much greater, the researchers say, because the numbers in this study do not include trips to doctors' offices, only hospital emergency rooms.

THE 2010 EARTHQUAKE IN HAITI THAT KILLED MORE THAN 200,000 PEOPLE INFLICTED ADDITIONAL PAIN ON INJURED HAITIANS FOR MONTHS AFTERWARD. WHY?

About three out of ten surgeries had to be redone because they occurred under poor conditions, in some cases by doctors working hastily and using inadequate equipment and supplies. To make matters worse, the surgeries were done in makeshift hospitals that were far from sterile, leading to postsurgical infections. **Bonus question: The devastation wrought by the earthquake in Haiti was exacerbated by shoddy construction of buildings throughout Port au Prince, its capital. What other cities are at similar risk?** Tehran, Iran, tops the list. Seismologists and others say an earthquake of the magnitude that struck Haiti could kill more than 1 million people in Tehran. Other at-risk cities include Lima, Peru; Istanbul, Turkey; Karachi, Pakistan; and Katmandu, Nepal.

WHAT PERCENTAGE OF AMERICANS OVER SIXTY-FIVE HAVE NO NATURAL TEETH?

Twenty-five. And that's about the percentage of Americans who have untreated cavities. The good news is Americans have done a better job of caring for their teeth in recent decades, and it's paid off. Today, nearly 40 percent of adults have never had to have a tooth pulled because of cavities or disease. Just fifteen years ago, only 30 percent of adults could make that claim. It's another story in India, where 67 percent of adults have never received dental care. In many developing nations, pulling a tooth is the only way to relieve pain. **Bonus question #1: Can bad teeth and gums cause heart attacks?** There's no proof of that, but recent research shows there is an association between the two. Infected gums release toxins that can move throughout the body, especially to the arteries, which can narrow—a key component of heart disease. **What you can do:** Most dentists say flossing is as important—or more important—than brushing, but that doesn't mean you can skip brushing. At a minimum, brush the front and back of each tooth for at least one second. And don't forget mouthwash. The kind that stings your mouth is best because it kills more germs.

IS THERE A CONNECTION BETWEEN THE OCCURRENCE OF HEADACHES AND THE WEATHER?

There is, according to one study, which found that more people seek treatment for severe headache pain when it's warmer. Hospital visits for headaches increased 7.5 percent for every increase of 9 degrees F. (The researchers found a much weaker link between headaches and barometric pressure and none at all between headaches and air pollution levels.) Why warm weather and headaches? No one seems to know.

WHAT'S THE BEST REMEDY FOR CHRONIC HEADACHES?

Would you believe acupuncture? In a series of studies, 62 percent of the participants found relief from acupuncture compared with 45 percent who credited medication. In other studies, 53 percent said acupuncture helped them while 45 percent felt better after taking a placebo. **What you can do:** Migraine symptoms tend to peak in the morning, particularly after 6:00 a.m., so take your medicine then or soon after you wake up.

IF YOU'RE AN ADULT TRYING TO DODGE THE FLU, WHAT MAKES MORE SENSE—GETTING A SHOT OF THE VACCINE OR GETTING THE NASAL SPRAY?

The former. In a study that looked at 1 million military members over a three-year period, trips to the doctor for flulike symptoms dropped 54 percent for those who received flu shots compared to 21 percent for those who received the nasal spray. The spray vaccine, which is increasingly popular among adults, is recommended for children, and some studies show it helps children more than shots.

AS MANY AS ONE-THIRD OF CHILDREN IN PUBLIC HOUSING SUFFER FROM ASTHMA. WHY?

A team of Boston University scientists blames cockroaches. The long-held theory that these children develop asthma from dust mites, dog dander, or pollen isn't true, say the scientists, who used vacuum cleaners to collect dust and discovered that it contains proteins from *Blattella germanica*—the common cockroach. These proteins are the true cause of these children's asthma.

WHO'S BETTER ABLE TO FUNCTION WELL WITHOUT SLEEP—THE OLD OR THE YOUNG?

The old. A study of thirty-seven healthy people—twenty-six younger than twenty-nine and eleven older than sixty-five—who were deprived of sleep for twenty-six hours found that the older folks were less likely to fall asleep and make common day-to-day mistakes.

And the seniors had faster reaction times. **What you can do:** Don't skimp on sleep. Doctors say most people need at least seven hours of sleep per night, and some as many as nine.

IT'S COMMON KNOWLEDGE THAT POOR HEALTH LEADS TO UNEMPLOYMENT, BUT DOES UNEMPLOYMENT LEAD TO POOR HEALTH?

It appears so. Healthy workers who lost their jobs were nearly twice as likely to develop a health condition, such as high blood pressure, as employed people, according to an analysis of data from 8,125 individuals. The results of this report provide more proof that stress—in this case, from losing a job and not being able to find another one—leads to sickness. **What you can do:** Doctors recommend that job seekers build exercise into their routines by spending at least thirty minutes three days a week working out in some capacity. And if you find yourself snacking more because you're at home, stick with fruits, vegetables, and nuts.

IT HAS BEEN NOTED THAT U.S. PRESIDENTS WHO ENTER OFFICE WITH BROWN OR BLACK HAIR LEAVE WITH GRAY. DOES STRESS MAKE US GRAY?

Stress may or may not be involved, but doctors know for sure that genetics play a big role. We know we get grayer as we get older. But why? A team of scientists discovered in 2009 that hydrogen peroxide, which hair cells produce a little at a time, accumulates in the root and prevents the natural pigment of hair from coloring the strand, leaving it gray. Scientists say this finding will help them determine if stress is a factor at all. **What you can do:** If genetics play as large a role in determining the color of our hair as scientists think, there may not be a lot you can do, but it couldn't hurt to try these things: (1) eat nutritious foods; deficiencies of nutrients, especially copper and B vitamins, may lead to early graying; (2) massage your scalp during shampooing to help nourish follicles; (3) stop smoking, which causes the body to age; (4) don't pluck; it does nothing but damage roots; and (5) see a doctor if you're graying prematurely and you don't have a family history of that. It could signal a health problem.

WHEN IT COMES TO WEIGHT, WHICH COUNTRY IS MOST LIKELY TO IGNORE DOCTORS' ADVICE, AND WHICH IS MOST LIKELY TO USE SMOKING AS A WEIGHT-LOSS STRATEGY?

Only 11 percent of Swiss said their doctors' urging provided a motivation to lose weight, while 29 percent of Americans and 46 percent of Mexicans cared about what their doctors said about weight loss. In Russia—more than in any other nation—21 percent said they smoke to keep off the weight while only 5 percent of Americans say that's why they smoke. Other tidbits from the poll include those most likely to use diet pills: Chinese (37 percent), followed by Brazilians (30 percent), Russians (24 percent), Mexicans (23 percent), and Americans (19 percent).

WHICH COUNTRY FEELS THE MOST PRESSURE TO LOSE WEIGHT, AND WHICH COUNTRY IS MOST LIKELY TO DO SOMETHING ABOUT IT?

Brazilians, who are famous for their skimpy bikinis, feel the most pressure to lose weight, and Finns have tried to lose weight more than those in other countries, according to a 2009 poll of 16,000 people in sixteen nations. To be exact, 83 percent of Brazilians think we put too much emphasis on weight, followed by Indians (68 percent), and Americans (62 percent). As for the dieters, 83 percent of Finns said they've tried a diet at least once, followed by the Dutch (73 percent), Australians (72 percent), and Americans (72 percent).

ARE OVERWEIGHT CHILDREN LESS LIKELY TO BE INJURED IN A CAR CRASH BECAUSE THEY HAVE MORE PADDING?

No, but they are more likely to suffer injuries to their arms and legs. Overweight or obese children were two and a half times more likely to injure their arms and legs, according to a study of 3,232 children ages nine to fifteen. The researchers don't know why exactly, but they theorize that the extra weight puts more stress on arms and legs upon impact. **Bonus question: What percentage of American children are obese?** Seventeen. **What you can do:** Obesity among children has become a huge problem in the United States. Doctors recommend children cut back on soda, juice, and between-meal snacks, exercise an hour a day, and watch less TV. In fact, studies show that children with TVs in their bedrooms sleep and exercise less and are more likely to snack more than children without TVs in their rooms.

ARE YOU MORE LIKELY TO BE FAT IF YOU LIVE NEAR A FAST-FOOD RESTAURANT?

Yes. A study of ninth graders and pregnant women found that the students were more likely to be obese and the women more likely to gain more weight the closer they lived to fast-food joints. Obesity rates were 5 percent higher for ninth graders whose schools were within a tenth of a mile of a pizza place or fast-food restaurant. And women were more likely to gain more than forty-four pounds during their pregnancies if they lived within a half mile of fast food. While academics praised the study, restaurateurs criticized it, saying it ignored the participants' overall diet and exercise. **Bonus question: About what percentage of Americans buy fast food at least once a month?** Eighty. **What you can do:** If you're addicted to fast food, dieticians and nutritionists say it's unlikely you can quit it cold turkey. Rather, limit yourself. Decide to eat fast food only once a week or once every two weeks rather than several days a week, as some people do.

DO FOOD ADS ON TV SIMPLY PROMOTE COMPETITION BETWEEN COMPANIES SELLING SIMILAR BRANDS, AS THE INDUSTRY HAS LONG CLAIMED, OR DO THE ADS CAUSE TV VIEWERS TO EAT MORE?

The latter, according to a recent study. Yale researchers gave groups of children—118 kids in all—bowls of goldfish crackers and then turned on a fourteen-minute cartoon. Some of the children saw food ads during commercial breaks while others saw ads for games. The children who watched food ads ate 45 percent more goldfish than did the other children.

IF I'M SLEEPING LESS, AM I EATING MORE?

It appears so, and that's not a good thing. Studies show chronic sleep deprivation messes with hormones that regulate appetite. Specifically, it increases levels of a hormone (ghrelin) that stimulates your appetite and decreases levels of a hormone (leptin) that helps you know when you're full. According to a study that surveyed 87,000 American adults, about 33 percent of those who slept fewer than six hours a night were obese. Of those who slept between six and nine hours, only 22 percent were obese. By the way, Americans spend an average of six hours and forty minutes sleeping per weekday night—down from ten hours before the lightbulb was invented. **What you can do:** People who sleep less don't usually eat more meals than those who sleep eight or more hours a day, but they snack more often. It's OK to nibble between meals if you're eating fruits and vegetables, but if you can't go a day without cookies and chips, doctors advise limiting yourself to one unhealthy snack per day.

WHICH IS THE MOST OBESE COUNTRY IN THE WORLD?

The Pacific Island nation of Nauru, where a whopping 79 percent of the population is obese. Next fattest are Tonga (56 percent) and French Polynesia (41 percent)—also in the Pacific—followed by Saudi Arabia (36 percent), United Arab Emirates (34 percent), and the United States (34 percent). Obese, by the way, is defined as a body mass index of 30 or more. Alabama, Mississippi, Tennessee, and West Virginia have the most obese people per capita in the United States, while Colorado has the least. **Not obese, but:** Overweight is a body mass index of 25 to 29.9, as defined by the World Health Organization and the U.S. Centers for Disease Control and Prevention. About 34 percent of Americans are overweight. That means nearly seven out of ten Americans are either obese or overweight.

OK, AMERICANS ARE FAT. BUT HOW FAT?

- Forty percent of men and 25 percent of women are too fat to enlist in the military, which spends about $60 million a year to recruit and train soldiers and sailors who are discharged because of weight problems.
- Airlines could save $250 million a year on jet fuel if we weren't obese, and motorists could save about $3 billion a year on gas.
- Twenty-nine percent of U.S. school districts have banned bake sales because of obesity-related regulations.
- Businesses collectively lose nearly $13 billion a year from absenteeism due to obesity.
- Obese Americans spend about $4,829 a year on health care—$1,429 more per year than those who are not obese.

What you can do: For starters, avoid "white" foods, such as bread, cookies, and cake, and satisfy your sweet tooth by eating lots of fruit. And substitute just about everything you drink with water or white milk.

IF YOU'RE TEN TO FIFTEEN POUNDS OVERWEIGHT, HOW MUCH ARE YOU HURTING YOURSELF?

Not at all. In fact, you may be helping yourself, according to recent studies, which found that people who are a little overweight are no more likely than normal weight people to die of cancer or heart disease. One study found a reduced risk of dying for slightly overweight people in their seventies, and others found that a little extra weight may strengthen bones and may help women look younger as they age. **Bonus question: What's brown fat, and why should you want it?** Brown fat is another name for baby fat, which burns energy and calories and helps babies stay warm. White fat tends to store energy and calories and, unlike brown fat, continues to develop as we age. Scientists are trying to figure out how to increase brown fat to help adults lose weight. **What you can do:** Many doctors, nutritionists, and trainers have come to believe that overweight people can be healthy and that eating healthy and exercising regularly are more important than a number on a scale.

WHAT'S MORE DANGEROUS TO YOUR HEALTH—SMOKING OR OBESITY?

Flip a coin. A forty-year study of 45,920 Swedish men found that men who were obese at eighteen were as likely to die at sixty as light smokers—defined as those who smoked one to ten cigarettes a day—but twice as likely to die at sixty as men who were not obese. **Bonus question: In what age range are Americans most likely to be obese?** Forty to fifty-nine. This happens to be the oldest group of Americans who were raised at a time when fast-food restaurants began popping up all over the country. Forty percent of all men and 41 percent of all women in that age bracket are obese, which is defined as having a body mass index of 30 or higher. This group has more obese people than those sixty and older for two reasons: People who are sixty and older weren't raised on fast food, and obese people over sixty don't live many more years so there are fewer of them around.

MOST PEOPLE HAVE HEARD THAT SMOKING CAN LEAD TO HEART DISEASE, AND THAT'S RIGHT: A SMOKER IS SIX TIMES MORE LIKELY THAN A NONSMOKER TO SUFFER FROM HEART PROBLEMS, MAKING IT THE TOP PREDICTOR FOR HEART DISEASE. WHICH IS THE SECOND-HIGHEST PREDICTOR?

It's low IQ scores. According to a study that tracked 1,145 men and women in Scotland for twenty years, those with low IQ scores were four times more likely to suffer from heart disease than those with higher IQ scores. In fact, a low IQ score was a higher predictor of heart disease than not exercising and high blood pressure. How could this be? The researchers theorize that factors that lead to low IQ also lead to poor heart health. After all, plenty of studies show that people with lower intelligence levels are more likely to adopt bad health-related habits, such as smoking, drinking too much alcohol, and eating poorly. Another somewhat controversial theory is that the heart, brain, and other organs of people with a high IQ function better and work more efficiently. **What you can do:** You don't have control over your IQ, but you do have control over how you treat your body. Cardiologists suggest the following tips to combat congestive heart failure: (1) limit your salt intake to less than 2,000 milligrams per day, (2) don't smoke, (3) eat sensible portions, (4) exercise regularly but don't overdo it, and (5) achieve your ideal weight. To find out what that is, go to the Centers for Disease Control and Prevention's website, or type "body mass index calculator" into Google or any search engine.

YOU'VE HEARD IT A MILLION TIMES: SMOKING CIGARETTES CAUSES CANCER, HEART DISEASE AND STROKE, JUST TO NAME THREE. CAN THERE POSSIBLY BE A DOWNSIDE TO QUITTING?

It appears so. It's widely known that smokers who quit often gain weight, but it's much less known that quitting also leads to an increased risk of developing type-2 diabetes. And longtime smokers are less likely to develop Parkinson's disease than nonsmokers. In the diabetes study, researchers followed 10,892 middle-aged smokers who did not have diabetes from 1987 to 1989. Those who quit increased by 70 percent their risk of developing diabetes for the first six years after they quit. Those who continued to smoke also increased their risk for developing diabetes—but by only 30 percent. The diabetes risk for smokers also increased, but when it comes to diabetes, food is a bigger danger than tobacco. The Parkinson's study, which included 305,468 people who were at least fifty years old, found that those who smoked for one to nine years were 4 percent less likely to develop the disease. But those who smoked for ten to nineteen years were 22 percent less likely to get Parkinson's, those who smoked for twenty to twenty-nine years were 36 percent less likely, and those who smoked for thirty years or more were 41 percent less likely to get it. The researchers said the number of cigarettes didn't matter as much as how long the people smoked. **What you can do:** Doctors caution you not to use any of this research as a reason to continue smoking. Quit, and whether or not you're at risk for diabetes or Parkinson's, watch your weight and make sure your doctor regularly checks you for both diseases.

HOW MANY PEOPLE SMOKE IN THE UNITED STATES, AND WHAT'S THE TREND?

About 46 million people, or 15 percent of the population, smoked in 2008—down from 50.1 million, or 26 percent of the population, in 1965. Back in 1965, two out of three smokers smoked fifteen or more cigarettes a day, but in 2008, only about two out of five smokers smoked fifteen or more cigarettes a day. **What you can do:** If you want to quit, here are some tips from doctors: (1) try staying away from other smokers; (2) cut down on alcohol; (3) use a nicotine oral inhaler, a nicotine patch, or nicotine gum; (4) consider psychotherapy if you're smoking for emotional reasons; (5) substitute water for cigarettes if you're smoking to try to lose weight.

IF YOU HAVE FRIENDS OR LOVED ONES WHO SMOKE AND YOU REALLY WANT THEM TO STOP, WILL IT HELP TO PAY THEM?

Apparently so. University of Pennsylvania researchers tracked 878 people and gave all of them information about programs to quit smoking. Then the researchers split the groups in two and offered only one money—as much as $750—to quit. At the end of the study, nearly 10 percent of those who were paid had quit, compared with only about 3.5 percent of the group that was offered no money.

IS THERE ONE CITY IN AMERICA THAT REALIZES THE DANGER OF SECONDHAND SMOKE MORE THAN THE OTHERS?

If there is, it's Pueblo, Colorado. In 2003, Pueblo banned smoking in public places and then local health officials did an experiment, tracking the number of heart attacks in Pueblo and comparing that number with the number of heart attacks in the county where Pueblo is located as well as in a nearby county. In the year and a half before the ban, heart attack rates were nearly identical and slowly declining in Pueblo and in those two counties. But eighteen months after the ban took effect, hospitalizations for heart attacks plummeted 27 percent in Pueblo but stayed the same in the two counties. After another eighteen months, hospitalizations had sunk 41 percent in Pueblo since before the smoking ban while hospitalizations in the counties hadn't changed. **Bonus question: What percentage of Americans live in a city or town where smoking has been banned in the workplace and/ or in restaurants?** About eighty. **What you can do:** Don't take secondhand smoke lightly. Hundreds of studies have come to the same conclusion: It's dangerous. So avoid it as much as you can. If you smoke, don't do it in the presence of others, and don't smoke indoors even if those you live with aren't around at the time.

WHAT PERCENTAGE OF DOCTORS IN CHINA SMOKE?

The answer: 56.8. In China, the world's largest tobacco consumer, more than 350 million people—nearly 40 percent of the population—smoke at least occasionally. The average Chinese smoker lights up sixteen times a day. Although China is urging its doctors to quit to set a good example for others, some of its government health officials smoke, even at official meetings. Antismoking advocates say curbing smoking in China will prove very difficult as long as the cheapest brands cost only ten cents per pack. **Bonus question: What percentage of American doctors smoke?** Three. However, American doctors are more likely to drink alcohol than the general public, but they are less likely to drink excessively.

WALKING IS GREAT EXERCISE, BUT HOW FAST DO YOU HAVE TO WALK TO REAP THE BEST BENEFITS?
At least one hundred steps a minute, according to a new study, which also measured heart rates. Those who walk at this rate five times a week for thirty minutes each reach a government recommended "moderate intensity" workout. Not only that, but a French study says the faster older adults walk, the less likely they are to die from heart disease. Slower walkers are three times more likely to suffer from cardiovascular disease. **What you can do:** Besides walking, here are some activities that trainers say fits the moderate-intensity bill: gardening, leisurely jogging, bike riding, and swimming as well as doubles tennis, ballroom and line dancing, and volleyball.

CHINA HAS INVESTED UNTOLD BILLIONS IN GREEN ENERGY TECHNOLOGY DURING THE PAST TWENTY YEARS, BUT IN 2006 IT PASSED THE UNITED STATES AS THE WORLD'S LARGEST PRODUCER OF GREENHOUSE GASES. JUST HOW BAD IS THE AIR POLLUTION IN BEIJING?
Really bad. An air monitor placed on the roof of one of the U.S. embassy's buildings in Beijing has registered a reading of 500, the highest rating it can give. In the United States, a reading of above 100 signifies unhealthy air. The highest-ever readings in America—in the 300 range—have only been taken downwind from forest fires.

AMERICANS ARE MORE EDUCATED ABOUT THE IMPORTANCE OF EXERCISING AND EATING RIGHT, SO WHAT HAVE THEY DONE WITH THAT KNOWLEDGE?
Mostly ignored it. During the past twenty years, the percentage of Americans between

forty and seventy-four who eat five fruits and vegetables a day has decreased from forty-two to twenty-six, the obesity rate has increased from 28 percent to at least 34 percent, and the percentage of people who work out at least thirty minutes three times a week has gone from about half to 43 percent.

SO, *YOU* MANAGE TO EAT HEALTHY AND FEED YOUR CHILDREN PLENTY OF FRUITS AND VEGETABLES. THAT MEANS THEY'LL GROW UP AND FOLLOW YOUR EXAMPLE, RIGHT?

Wrong. A new study of 2,291 parents and 2,692 children shows that children are more likely to be influenced by their peers' eating habits than by their parents'. This was true regardless of the parents' education level or the family's socioeconomic status.

WHICH COUNTRIES HAVE THE MOST UNDERNOURISHED PEOPLE?

Seventy-five percent of the population of Eritrea, in East Africa, is undernourished, followed by the Congo (74 percent) and the East African nation of Burundi (66 percent). **Bonus question #1: What are the chances that a child in the United States will depend on food stamps at some point in his or her life?** One in two.

IN 1971, PRESIDENT RICHARD NIXON SAID WE SHOULD CURE CANCER BY 1976. HOW ARE WE DOING ON THAT GOAL?

Lousy. The death rate from cancer—slightly fewer than 200 deaths per year per 100,000 people—dropped only 5 percent from 1950 to 2005. Lung cancer death rates have soared for women, who appear to be at greater risk for it for reasons that are unclear, and death rates for other cancers have either increased or decreased only slightly. Why? Researchers say Nixon and most of the medical world underestimated how difficult it would be to find a cure. The good news, they say, is that we have made advances in cancer treatment, especially when the cancer doesn't spread.

DO CANCER PATIENTS IN SUPPORT GROUPS LIVE LONGER THAN THOSE WHO DON'T RECEIVE SUPPORT?

A groundbreaking study in 1989 said yes, that women with breast cancer in support groups lived eighteen months longer than breast cancer sufferers going it alone. But the same researchers updated their study nearly twenty years later and found that's not the case. They concluded that those in support groups coped better but didn't live longer than those without support. The updated study is one of many that cast doubt on the practical benefits of positive thinking. **What you can do:** Don't stop attending support groups. Go for the emotional benefits they provide, but don't assume they'll contribute to lengthening your life.

IF YOU SUFFERED A STROKE, YOU'D KNOW IT, RIGHT?

Not necessarily. Researchers asked about 700 people ages sixty-five or older if they'd ever had a stroke. Eighty-five of them said yes, but 225 had signs of a stroke on brain scans. Were the others lying? The researchers say very few may have been, but most had a very minor stroke and never realized they had one and were never treated for it. Others had memory and language deficiencies and either didn't recall that they had a stroke or were unable to communicate that to the researchers. Other stroke victims who said they didn't have a stroke also suffered a heart attack.

WHO NAPS MORE: THE EMPLOYED OR THE UNEMPLOYED?

Thirty-nine percent of unemployed people and 31 percent of those with jobs say they take a nap each day, according to a 2009 survey of 1,488 adults. More men (38 percent) than women (31 percent) nap every day. More African Americans (50 percent) nap compared with whites (32 percent) and Hispanics (33 percent). Those who make less than $30,000 a year are more likely to nap than those who earn more. About one in three people in their twenties through seventies nap every day, but slightly more than half of those age eighty and older nap daily. In this survey, a nap was defined as sleeping a few minutes, a few hours, or anything in between. **What you can do:** Researchers who've worked with athletes, astronauts, and others have found that sometimes naps are just what we need to make it through the day, but timing is everything. Try to nap early in the afternoon if your schedule allows. A nap any later than that may disrupt your night-time sleep schedule.

OXYTOCIN, A HORMONE PRODUCED BY THE PITUITARY GLAND, IS BEST KNOWN FOR REGULATING BODILY FUNCTIONS, SUCH AS A WOMAN'S ABILITY TO DELIVER MILK TO HER BABY. WHY SHOULD YOU WANT YOUR BUSINESS PARTNER TO TAKE IT?

A growing body of research shows that an elevated level of the hormone caused people to trust each other more. In one study, twenty-nine male students received oxytocin via a nasal spray before playing a game created to test their tolerance for being betrayed by others, and twenty-nine others received a nasal spray without the hormone. The students who received the oxytocin were twice as likely to trust their partners during the game.

WHAT CAN YOU BUY FOR TWO CENTS THESE DAYS?

Two pennies will buy you a vitamin A tablet in developing nations, where vitamin A deficiency is the leading cause of preventable blindness in children. Nearly 500,000 children a year go blind because they don't consume enough of the vitamin, which is found in eggs, milk, spinach, carrots, and other foods. **What you can do:** Set aside about a month's worth of your loose change. Then donate it to UNICEF, the World Health Organization, the Canadian International Development Agency, USAID, or another organization that is working to make sure people in developing nations have enough vitamin A.

A donation of $36.50—ten cents a day—will buy enough vitamin A for a family of five for a year.

HOW ABOUT THREE CENTS?

Three cents can buy enough medicine to prevent someone from getting elephantiasis for a year. Also known as lymphatic filariasis, elephantiasis, which causes body parts to become disfiguringly swollen and infects more than 120 million people worldwide, is one of several worm-caused diseases crippling people in undeveloped nations. Other diseases include roundworm, also known as ascariasis (affecting about 807 million), whipworm, or trichuriasis, (more than 600 million), hookworm (more than 570 million), schistosomiasis (200 million), trachoma (about 70 million), and onchocerciasis (about 35 million). **What you can do:** Go to GlobalNetwork.org/just50cents. That's the web page for Global Network's campaign to raise money to combat these seven diseases. Fifty cents pays for a year's worth of medicine to prevent all seven of those diseases from infecting one person. Other organizations working on this problem include World Health Organization, Children Without Worms, and Deworm the World. Visit their websites to learn more.

Two

LIFE AND DEATH— BUT MOSTLY DEATH

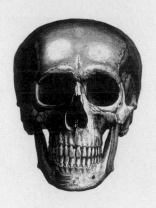

You may think you know what this chapter's about, but the facts in it are anything but predictable. You'll learn how many serial killers are on the loose in America at any given time, what the most common last words uttered by death-row prisoners are, what you can do if the airplane you're riding in fails, and why women live longer than men. You'll also find out which are the most dangerous days of the year to drive and to be a pedestrian, which states have the highest and lowest abortion rates and where the most dangerous place in the world to be an albino is.

OF THE 446 MEN AND WOMEN WHO HAVE BEEN EXECUTED IN TEXAS SINCE 1976, WHEN THE SUPREME COURT REINSTATED THE DEATH PENALTY, WHAT WAS THE MOST COMMON WORD USED IN THEIR LAST-WORDS SPEECHES?

Love, by far. Love was said 630 times, followed by thanks (243 times), sorry (211), God (175), death (132), Lord (130), life (126), peace (95), Jesus and mom (both 86), pray (80), warden (74), kill (69), ready (65), innocent (45), Allah (41), heaven (40), closure (20), fear (14), regret (12), deserve (10), guilty (7), hell (6), not guilty (4), and afraid (1).

KILLER COWS?

Yes, killer cows. They exist, and they are to be feared. Cows killed twenty-one people from 2003 to 2008 in Iowa, Missouri, Nebraska, and Kansas, and in sixteen of those cases, the animal—more likely to be a bull than a cow—did it on purpose. Of the twenty-one victims, twenty died from head or chest injuries. The other person died after the cow knocked him down. A syringe in his pocket stuck him, killing him with an antibiotic intended for the cow. **What you can do:** If you're at a petting zoo or otherwise near a cow, remember that they can act unpredictably. Respect their power and strength and keep your distance.

WHICH IS THE MOST DANGEROUS DAY OF THE YEAR TO DRIVE A CAR?

The Fourth of July is the day with the most traffic fatalities, with an average of 161, followed by July 3 (149) and December 23 and New Year's Day (both 145). Plain and simple, there's more driving and drinking alcohol around the holidays. New Year's Day might top this unfortunate list if not for the multitude of drinking and driving warnings broadcast as the holiday approaches and for the increased roadside sobriety checkpoints on New Year's Eve. **What you can do:** Avoid becoming a statistic by not drinking and driving, or drink a glass of water after every bottle of beer or glass of wine you consume. Water dulls the effect of the alcohol.

HOW ABOUT FOR PEDESTRIANS?

For pedestrians, New Year's Day is the deadliest, with 410 fatalities, and then Halloween, with 401. These holidays see more people than usual walking the streets, and in the early hours of New Year's Day, police point out, pedestrians are just as likely as drivers to be drunk, and sometimes their negligence leads to their demise.

WHAT PERCENTAGE OF STUDENTS SAID CHOKING YOURSELF IN AN ATTEMPT TO GET HIGH POSES NO RISK?

Forty percent, according to a survey of more than 2,500 middle and high school students in Texas and Canada. The fact is at least eighty-two children ages eleven to sixteen have died doing the so-called choking game, which involves temporarily cutting off the flow of oxygen to the brain in an attempt to reach a high. Public health officials believe many additional deaths from the same cause have been incorrectly ruled suicides. This study and one involving 10,642 students in Oregon found that about 6 percent of students have tried to do this. **What you can do:** Children with substance abuse problems are more likely to try this. Be aware of the warning signs: bloodshot eyes, headaches, and neck bruises.

HUMANS CAN TOLERATE AN AWFUL LOT OF ABUSE, BUT WHAT ARE OUR LIVE-OR-DIE LIMITS?

A 150-pound man can survive without food for forty-five days and without water for seven. He can survive in 40-degree water for no more than thirty minutes and in a 300-degree burning building for ten. He can survive a body temperature of no more than 107.6 degrees and no more than 40 percent blood loss. And while most people pass out if they're deprived of oxygen for two minutes, some can be trained to do without it for nearly eleven.

IN A RECENT SURVEY OF 1,007 AMERICAN ADULTS, 82 PERCENT SAID THEY WOULD SURVIVE JUST FINE IF A WINTER STORM KNOCKED OUT THEIR POWER AND MADE IT IMPOSSIBLE TO LEAVE HOME FOR TWO WEEKS. WHAT PERCENTAGE HAD ALL OF THE NECESSARY ITEMS TO LIVE COMFORTABLY?
One. And about half of those surveyed had fewer than ten of the sixteen things deemed to be important in a home emergency kit. According to the survey, 90 percent had a flashlight and over-the-counter fever reducers and pain relievers; 88 percent, a manual can opener; 83 percent, personal hygiene items; 80 percent, a first aid kit; 79 percent, a two-week supply of prescription drugs; 78 percent, extra batteries; 76 percent, a thermometer; 68 percent, hand sanitizer with at least 60 percent alcohol; 66 percent, a portable, battery-operated radio; 57 percent, a two-week supply of nonperishable food; 46 percent, nonprescription diarrhea drugs; 34 percent, a two-week supply of drinking water for each family member and chemical cold packs; 33 percent, electrolyte drinks such as Gatorade; and 14 percent, surgical masks with a rating of N-95 or higher. Nonprescription diarrhea drugs? Surgical masks? Hard to believe that 1 percent of households had all of those things. **What you can do:** Buy these items and keep them in a dry place.

WHAT ARE THE ODDS OF DYING IN A CAR CRASH VERSUS ON A ROLLER COASTER?
The odds are 40,000 to 1. If this is the case, why do we scream when we're riding on a roller coaster but not when we're riding down the highway? Risk assessors say we, like our ancestors, fear immediate threats (incredibly steep hills) more than abstract ones (sleepy truck drivers).

IF YOU'RE ON AN AIRPLANE THAT FAILS IN MIDAIR, WHAT ARE THE CHANCES THAT YOU'LL SURVIVE?
You have a .00132 percent chance of survival, according to the Geneva-based Aircraft Crashes Record Office. In all, 118,934 people have died in 15,463 crashes between 1940 and 2008. Only 157 have survived, including forty-two people who were in

planes that broke down above 10,000 feet. **Bonus question: Who has the best chance to survive plane crashes—adults or children?** Children. No one's sure why, but here are a few theories: They have flexible skeletons, more fat to protect organs, and their heads don't stick up above seatbacks, which shield them from flying debris inside the plane. In a crash in 2009 near the Comoros Islands in the Indian Ocean, a Yemeni passenger jet flying through bad weather crashed with 153 people aboard, and one passenger, a fourteen-year-old girl, survived. In 2010, a Libyan plane crashed in Libya, killing 103, mostly Dutch tourists. The sole survivor? A nine-year-old Dutch boy, whose worst injuries were badly broken legs. **What you can do:** It's never a bad idea to pray, but other than that, there isn't much you can do. However, "wreckage riders"—people who hang on to pieces of debris during their freefall or who remain strapped into their seats on the way down—sometimes (OK, rarely) have their falls partially broken by what they're holding on to or by their seats.

WHAT COLOR IS AN AIRPLANE'S FLIGHT DATA RECORDER, OR "BLACK BOX"?

Not black. It's bright orange so it can be more easily found in wreckage. And the paint is heat resistant. So why is it called a black box? No one seems to know for sure, but here's the most popular theory: The earliest film-based flight data recorders required the inside to be perfectly dark, like a photographer's darkroom, to prevent light from corrupting the record.

HOW MANY PEOPLE DIE EVERY YEAR IN THE UNITED STATES BECAUSE A DOCTOR, NURSE OR OTHER CAREGIVER MAKES A MISTAKE, AND WHAT ARE HOSPITALS DOING ABOUT IT?

Errors lead to somewhere between 44,000 and 98,000 deaths a year, and while most hospitals are working to reduce those numbers, a growing number are providing counseling to staffers who make life-ending errors as they would treat traumatized patients in need of care. A federal advisory group, called the National Quality Forum, has developed a program to treat these staffers whose errors lead to patients' deaths. **Bonus question: How many people die every year due to hospital infections?** About 100,000.

HOW MANY SERIAL KILLERS AND SERIAL KILLINGS ARE THERE IN THE UNITED STATES EVERY YEAR?

Criminologists guess there are about one hundred serial killers who have not been caught in the United States at any given time and as many as 1,800 homicides per year for which serial killers are responsible. The latter number is much higher than previously thought, but it's reasonable. About 100,000 missing-person cases remain open at any given time in the United States, and as many as 20,000 of those cases may be homicides. **Bonus question: What have scientists recently discovered about psychopaths?** Previous research has tried to explain psychopathic behavior by focusing on what psychopaths lack—fear, compassion, sensitivity, empathy, and interpersonal skills. New research says psychopaths have brains that are wired to seek reward. In tests in which they were offered money to complete tasks, researchers found psychopaths released large amounts of dopamine, a brain chemical most closely associated with pleasure and excitement.

WHAT PERCENTAGE OF ALL IDENTIFIABLE GUNS RECOVERED FROM CRIME SCENES IN MEXICO CAN BE TRACED TO U.S. GUN SHOPS?

Ninety. Gun control advocates blame states with laws that make it easy to buy guns. Mississippi has the highest rate of gun exports connected to crimes committed in the United States, per capita, followed by West Virginia, Alabama, Virginia, and South Carolina. When you look at total gun-related crimes committed in the States, Florida leads the way, followed by Virginia, Texas, and Indiana.

WHICH COUNTRIES HAVE THE LOWEST AND HIGHEST INFANT-MORTALITY RATES, AND WHERE DOES THE UNITED STATES RANK?

Singapore has the lowest rate—2.4 deaths per 1,000 births—followed by Sweden (2.5), Finland (2.7), and Japan (2.8). At 163 deaths per 1,000 births, Afghanistan has the highest, while Sierra Leone (158) and Liberia (133) are next highest. The United States was at 6.6 in 2008, the year for which the most recent worldwide data is available.

WHICH COUNTRIES HAVE THE LOWEST AND HIGHEST FERTILITY RATES?

The average number of children born to a woman in Macao and Hong Kong is 1.0, followed by 1.1 in Taiwan. The fertility rate in the West African nations of Niger and Guinea-Bissau is 7.1, while the number is 6.8 in Afghanistan, the nation with the world's highest infant-mortality rate. The fertility rate in the United States is slightly above 2.

HOW MANY CHILDREN WILL DIE PER YEAR FROM 2009 TO 2015 BECAUSE OF THE GLOBAL ECONOMIC CRISIS, WHICH BEGAN IN 2008?

About 200,000—or one every two minutes and forty-three seconds—is the best-case scenario. About 400,000—or one every one minute and nineteen seconds—is the worst-case scenario.

ABORTION RATES HAVE DROPPED SHARPLY SINCE 1990. WHICH STATES HAVE THE HIGHEST AND LOWEST RATES?

With its large numbers of young, single people, Washington, DC, at 54.2, has the highest rate per 1,000 women between fifteen and forty-four. Wyoming has the lowest rate, at .7. When you look at race, black women have the highest rate (49.7) and white women the lowest (13.8).

IN WHAT YEAR WERE THE MOST BABIES BORN IN THE UNITED STATES?

In 2007, about 4,317,000 babies were born, just surpassing the number in 1957, the year when the most Baby Boomers were born. What happened in 1957, however, was more significant, demographers say, because the average woman then gave birth to slightly more than three children. In 2007, the average woman gave birth to two children. The record number of births in 2007 is simply a result of a large number of women of childbearing age. **Bonus question: What's expected to happen as a result of the '57 boom?** In 2020, when the 1957 babies turn sixty-three, the United States is expected to have a shortage of 85,000 doctors, specifically surgeons, oncologists, cardiologists, and primary care physicians. So if you thought you were waiting a long time to see your doctor now, just wait.

LIFE EXPECTANCY IN THE UNITED STATES CONTINUES TO INCREASE FOR ALL SEXES AND RACES, BUT WHICH GROUP HAS MADE THE BIGGEST STRIDES SINCE 1970?

Black males. Overall, life expectancy has soared from 70.8 years in 1970 to 77.9 years in 2007. Broken down by sex, that's 75.3 years for men and 80.4 years for women. White women lived the longest in 1970 (75.6) and they still do (80.8), but they've made shorter strides since 1970 than have white males, who live 7.7 years longer now than in 1970; black females, who live 8.2 years longer now; and black males, who live 9.5 years longer now. **What you can do:** You can't do anything about your genes, but geriatric physicians say those who live past their average lifespan have one thing in common: They keep physically and mentally active—walking and swimming, reading and playing bridge, crossword puzzles, and musical instruments. Case in point: Supreme Court Justice John Paul Stevens was born in 1920 and had a life expectancy of 57.5 years, giving him until 1977 to kick the bucket. Stevens, who has since retired from the Court, is an avid tennis player. He turned ninety in 2010.

HOW MUCH LONGER CAN WE EXPECT TO LIVE IF THE AIR WE BREATHE IS CLEAN?
Five months, according to a study that examined life expectancy and air quality improvements in fifty-one U.S. metropolitan areas from the early 1980s to the late 1990s. In those places, air quality improved, and life expectancy rose two years and eight months. The researchers credit cleaner air to five months of that.

THE VAST MAJORITY OF SUPERCENTENARIANS—PEOPLE 110 AND OLDER—ARE WOMEN. WHY?
In 2009, sixty-eight of the known seventy-two supercentenarians were women. Here are five theories: (1) young men are five times as likely to die in an accident; (2) estrogen increases the level of good cholesterol and decreases the level of bad cholesterol; testosterone works in reverse; (3) men are five times more likely to die by firearms; (4) men are more likely to die of heart disease and cancer; and (5) men are more likely to ignore signs of depression. In fact, older men, between seventy-five and seventy-nine, are nine times more likely than women to commit suicide. **Bonus question: Getting to 110 is practically impossible, but making it to 100 is becoming more and more likely as doctors figure out how to keep folks alive longer. How many centenarians are living in the United States?** About 79,000.

FOR YEARS, PSYCHOLOGISTS HAVE TALKED UP HOW SUNSHINE MAKES US HAPPIER, BUT IS THAT ALWAYS SO?
No, not in Greenland, which has one of the world's highest suicide rates. Suicides there have been blamed on high unemployment and rampant alcoholism. And a new study found that most of the suicides occur in the summer in the part of the country north of the Arctic Circle where the sun remains above the horizon for four months. All of that sun, researchers say, makes it harder to sleep and may disrupt the flow of serotonin, a brain chemical that regulates moods.

WHICH COUNTRY USES THE DEATH PENALTY MORE THAN ANY OTHER?

China, by far. In 2008, China reported executing 1,718 people—72 percent of all the death-penalty executions in the world that year. Iran came in second with 346, followed by Saudi Arabia (102), the United States (37), Pakistan (36) and Iraq (34). In all, twenty-five of the fifty-nine nations that have death sentences on the books reported 2,390 executions that year. The others executed no one that year.

AT LEAST NINE NATIONS HAVE NUCLEAR WEAPONS. WHICH ARE MOST LIKELY TO USE THEM AGAINST EACH OTHER, AND WHAT WOULD HAPPEN TO THE ENVIRONMENT IF THEY DID?

Iran is the biggest wild card, but most experts say India, with about fifty warheads, and Pakistan, with about sixty, are most likely to use their weapons against each other. If those two nations used a total of one hundred warheads, the consequences would greatly exceed any damage man has ever done to Earth. Within forty-nine days, soot from the ensuing fires would block enough of the sun that Earth would be overcast everywhere, causing a global agricultural collapse. As many as 1 billion people with marginal food supplies could die as a result. The particles in the smoke that rise into the stratosphere, where there is no rain, could take ten years to settle to Earth.

HOW MANY AMERICAN LIVES ARE SAVED PER MONTH WHEN GASOLINE COSTS $4 PER GALLON OR MORE?

One thousand. Gas has cost $4 per gallon for decades in parts of Europe and elsewhere, but when it hit $4 per gallon in the United States in the summer of 2008, drivers reacted by staying home more, and less driving resulted in fewer fatal car accidents. For every 10 percent rise in gas prices, fatalities are reduced by 2.3 percent, one researcher said. **Bonus question: What role, if any, do higher speed limits have on vehicle fatalities?** Fatalities rose 3.2 percent a year starting in 1995, the year the national highway speed limit of 55 mph was raised everywhere. As of 2010, thirty-four states have highway speed limits of 70 mph or more. Of those, New Mexico, Idaho, and Nevada have maximum speed limits of 75 mph.

HOW CAN ICE SAVE YOUR LIFE?

The Greek physician Hippocrates, the namesake of the Hippocratic oath, advocated packing wounded soldiers in snow and ice, and a growing number of studies report positive results in using ice to treat heart attack victims whose hearts stop beating for several minutes or more. The treatment, called therapeutic hypothermia, begins after the heartbeat is restored, when ice is packed around the head and body in an attempt to lower the patient's body temperature by about 6 degrees. (Intravenous fluids may also be used to cool the body.) Lowering the body temperature protects the brain from some of the effects of oxygen deprivation. Doctors then use drugs to induce a twenty-four-hour coma before returning the body to its normal temperature. It seems like a lot of trouble, but survival rates using this treatment are much better. **Bonus question: How long can someone be dead before being revived with a treatment involving ice?** A Brooklyn man was dead for forty-seven minutes in August 2009 before emergency room doctors used ice and other treatments, including 4,500 chest compressions, to revive him.

HOW CLOSE CAN WE GET TO THE SUN BEFORE WE'D DIE?

About halfway there. The sun is about 93 million miles away from us, and the intense radiation would kill us by the time we traveled about 47 million miles of it. If we had a shield that protected us from all of that nasty radiation, we could get a lot closer, like about 1.3 million miles from the sun. NASA's existing space shuttle's heat shield will hold up to 4,700 degrees F, but it degrades quickly when it gets hotter than that. And the sun is much hotter. Its surface, the coolest part of the star, is about 9,940 degrees.

Three

HOW MUCH DID SOMEONE ACTUALLY PAY FOR A COW NAMED MISSY?

Money happens to be one of the most universal topics of conversation including now and in history. Jesus spoke more about money than about anything else, even everlasting life. This chapter answers dozens of money-related questions, including these: What percent of people who make more than $100,000 a year live paycheck to paycheck? Why do the poor pay more for groceries than the middle and upper classes? What's the most anyone's ever spent on a penny, on a white truffle, or on lunch? How do Vegas casinos spy on you? What positive things occur during recessions, and what lousy yet surprising things occur?

IF YOU HAD $10,000 TO INVEST ON OCTOBER 1, 1964, WHAT SHOULD YOU HAVE DONE WITH IT?
If you gave it to Warren Buffett to invest in Berkshire Hathaway, that $10,000—the

equivalent of about $70,000 today—would be worth $80 million. How about the two most successful mutual funds of the past fifty years? If you invested in Fidelity Magellan, you'd have $9.1 million, and you'd have about $2.9 million if you put your money in Templeton Growth. You'd have about $560,000, by the way, if you put your ten grand in the Standard and Poor's 500, an index of 500 widely held stocks viewed as a benchmark for how the stock market is doing. Why the disparity? Mutual fund managers face more short-term pressures and typically don't hold a stock as long as they might. And the S&P 500 is so large that losses often neutralize gains. **What you can do:** If you have $10,000, most financial advisors suggest you use it to pay off your debt, then if there's anything left over, buy a mutual fund that believes in diversifying.

WANT TO MAKE MONEY OFF HURRICANES?
Three stocks consistently rose right before and after the most destructive hurricanes in modern U.S. history—Campbell Soup Company, Nucor Corporation and Hill-Rom Holdings. Campbell benefits from people stocking up on soup as they prepare for hurricanes, Nucor provides steel for large steel projects, and Hill-Rom makes hospital beds and medical equipment, which are in demand during the aftermath of hurricanes.

HOW MUCH DOES IT COST TO MAKE A PENNY AND A NICKEL?
Two and nine cents, respectively, and that fact has caused a lot of people, including President Obama, to say we need to do it in a more cost-effective way. At stake is $100 million a year—the cost to use cheaper materials, though the government hasn't said what it would use instead. A penny, by the way, isn't made of copper, and a nickel doesn't contain very much nickel. A nickel is made mostly of copper, and a penny is mostly zinc. And it's the zinc lobbyists, many of whom represent Canadian mining companies, who are fighting the change the hardest.

WHAT'S THE MOST ANYONE HAS PAID FOR A PENNY?

At an auction in 2009, someone paid nearly $1.3 million, including commissions, for a 1795 reeded-edge U.S. penny, one of seven known to exist. That sale marked the first time someone paid more than $1 million for a one-cent coin.

WHAT'S ABOUT THE CHEAPEST AIRFARE YOU CAN GET SHORT OF FREE?

As part of a "Take Me Away" promotion in 2009, AirAsia advertised a one-way fare of twenty-six cents to fly from the Malaysia cities of Kuala Lumpur to Penang—a 181-mile flight, roughly the same distance between New York City and Baltimore.

WHAT'S MORE—3 DOLLARS OR 300 CENTS?

Three hundred cents. Psychology researchers have found that people will make decisions based on numbers that seem larger but aren't necessarily so. A recent experiment led by Ohio State University researchers rewarded those who participated the most in a test known as the prisoner's dilemma, in which two people are offered incentives to work together or defect. The level of cooperation increased when the reward went from 3 cents to 300 cents but not when it went from 3 cents to 3 dollars. The results of this experiment mirrored other similar studies. **Bonus question: What's more—two $100 bills or 200 $1 bills?** *200 One Dollar Bills.* Two hundred $1 bills are worth $200; *200 One Dollar Bills* is worth $43.8 million. At least that's what someone paid in 2009 for the Andy Warhol 7.5-foot-wide silkscreen, *200 One Dollar Bills.* The London-based art collector who sold it paid $385,000 for it in 1986. **What you can do:** Save your loose change. People who never spend their loose change accumulate anywhere from $125 to $350 a year.

WHAT WILL SOME FOLKS DO FOR $5?

Give break-dance lessons, write an Italian love song, revise résumés, edit PowerPoint presentations, and translate Chinese words into English, among other tasks. These $5 gigs and more have been offered on a website called Fiverr.com, run out of Israel, which gives $4 to the person offering the service and keeps a $1 commission. If some of these deals seem too good to be true, chalk it up to a lousy economy, in which a lot of talented people are doing whatever they can to make some money.

IF YOU BOUGHT A TYPEWRITER FOR $50 IN 1963, WHAT WOULD IT BE WORTH IN 2009?

Try $254,500. That's what an anonymous American collector paid for an Olivetti type-writer owned by award-winning novelist Cormac McCarthy, who used the light blue manual machine to type all of his books. The proceeds—after the auction house's commission—will go to the Santa Fe Institute, a nonprofit interdisciplinary scientific research organization. After McCarthy handed the typewriter over to be sold, a friend bought him an identical typewriter for less than $20. **What you can do:** If you're at an auction, remember this: People bid more when they're sitting on soft chairs. That's according to researchers who found that buyers at car auctions bid an average of $1,243.60 more than they planned when sitting on soft chairs. Those on hard chairs bid $896.50 more than they planned. The researchers attribute this to our sense of touch, which can cause us to do things we wouldn't otherwise do.

WHAT PERCENTAGE OF AMERICAN PAPER MONEY CONTAINS TRACES OF COCAINE?

Ninety. That far exceeds the percentage (67) from a study in 2007. The 2009 study, which came up with the 90 percent figure, found that $5, $10, $20, and $50 bills contained more cocaine than $1 and $100 bills and that 95 percent of the bills from Washington, DC, contained cocaine compared with 80 percent of the currency in Brazil and 20 percent in China. However, the researchers made it clear that 90 percent of all American paper currency is not used to snort cocaine. Rather, cocaine powder spreads easily through bill-counting machines. **What you can do:** Money, whether paper or coins, is touched by so many people it's always considered filthy. Try to wash your hands after handling it.

WHEN IT COMES TO CARS, WHY IS $25,000 CONSIDERED A MAGIC NUMBER?

That's the price that consumers who aren't interested in budget models feel they can afford to spend on a new car, according to automakers. The $25,000 level is attractive to buyers because it often translates to a doable monthly car payment of between $400 and $500, after trade-in or a 20 percent down payment. **What you can do:** If you feel like you can afford $25,000 for a new car, shop for models that cost between $20,000 and $22,000. After you add on fees, taxes and an option or two, your car may cost that much.

RECESSIONS ARE SCARY THINGS, BUT DO THEY HAVE AN UPSIDE?

Yes. Death rates fall during a recession. We smoke less, drink less, exercise more, and stay home more. While we're at home, we have more time to prepare meals, which tend to be healthier than the ones we order in restaurants. Healthier eating leads to fewer heart attacks. We also drive less, and because of that, there are fewer traffic fatalities. Less business activity during recessions means fewer on-the-job accidents and less pollution. Credit card debt decreases. Buying fewer things also means we generate less trash, and that lengthens the lives of landfills. College enrollment grows as the unemployed seek to make themselves more marketable. Thrift, craft, and grocery store sales increase.

ANYTHING ELSE GOOD COME OUT OF RECESSIONS?

More people eat candy, so candy stores do well. (Candy stores rarely went out of business even during the Great Depression.) And when the world seems to be crumbling around us, we don't want to go it alone. Divorce rates drop, and matchmaking services report brisk business. Oh, yeah, and tinsel makers say their business is brisk when times are tough. They say consumers return to simple and inexpensive decorations during recessions.

SO, BESIDES THE OBVIOUS, WHAT'S THE DOWNSIDE OF A RECESSION?

Lots of pet owners decide they can't afford their dogs and cats, and they send them to animal shelters in increased numbers. Unemployed people don't sleep well, and they buy more over-the-counter sleep aids. Suicide rates increase, as do cases of depression.

THE NUMBER OF PEOPLE WHO RELY ON FOOD STAMPS ALSO RISES DURING RECESSIONS. WHERE IN THE UNITED STATES DO THE MOST PEOPLE RECEIVE FOOD STAMPS?

Forty-nine percent of the people in Wade Hampton County, Alaska; Owsley County, Kentucky; and Shannon County, South Dakota, received food stamps in 2009. Some of the places where people use the most food stamps per capita are rural counties in either the South or in the Dakotas. Of cities or counties where 750,000 or more people live, the biggest food stamp users (29 percent of the population) are the Bronx, New York, and Hidalgo County, Texas. This doesn't mean that everyone who needs food stamps is getting them. California enrolls only about half of the people who are eligible for them. **And the least?** Less than 1 percent of those who live in Glasscock County, Texas, and Fairfax, Virginia, use food stamps.

WHEN TIMES ARE TOUGH, MORE PEOPLE CLIP COUPONS. WHO'S MOST LIKELY TO USE THEM?

Women, especially those under fifty-four with college degrees and household incomes above $70,000 a year. Coupon usage soared 27 percent—from 2.6 billion in 2008 to 3.3 billion in 2009—the largest increase since coupon usage was first tracked in the late

1980s. **What you can do:** If you use coupons, expect to save from $10 to $40 per week—or about $500 to $2,000 per year. Here are a few sites that serious coupon users love: HotCouponWorld.com, AFullCup.com, and CouponMom.com.

EVERYONE KNOWS VEGAS CASINOS USE OVERHEAD CAMERAS TO SEE WHAT THEIR GUESTS ARE UP TO, BUT WHAT ELSE DO THEY DO TO GATHER INFORMATION?

More than you'd ever guess. Many casinos use license plate readers that grab an image of your plate and run your history before you get out of your car. Cards printed with invisible bar codes keep cheaters from introducing their own cards into the game they're playing. Some casinos hide radio transmitters in their chips to confirm that cashed-in chips are not counterfeit. Casinos can also track the betting patterns and spending habits—down to what gamblers like to eat and drink—of patrons who use so-called customer-loyalty cards. **What you can do:** Don't even consider trying to cheat when you're at a casino. Go there with a limit of how much you plan to lose—er, spend—and don't exceed that limit.

WHAT'S THE MOST ANYONE HAS LOST GAMBLING IN LAS VEGAS?

This is a tough one to answer definitively, but put your money on Nebraska businessman Terrance Watanabe, who lost $127 million gambling at Rio and Caesars Palace casinos in 2007. That staggering amount comes to 5.6 percent of all the gambling revenue that Harrah's Entertainment, Inc., the two casinos' parent company, took in that year. Watanabe, who ran his family's party-favor business, paid about $112 million of his debt but refused to pay the rest. In a lawsuit he filed against Harrah's, he alleged that casino workers loaded him up with free alcoholic beverages and allowed him to gamble while drunk, a violation of casino protocol and Nevada law. The company said Watanabe had to take responsibility for his actions. In 2010, with the case nearing a trial, Watanabe dropped the lawsuit and agreed to have an arbitrator decide on a settlement that will be binding.

WHAT DOES IT COST TO STATION ONE U.S. SOLDIER IN AFGHANISTAN?
Nearly $1 million. Nearly half of that goes toward transporting soldiers and equipment. About 12.5 percent is to repair or replace damaged gear, 12 percent is to buy armor and armored vehicles, 11.4 percent is to train Afghans, 5.75 percent is for intelligence costs, and the rest is for construction, coalition support, research, and training Pakistanis.

IT'S AN UNDERSTATEMENT TO SAY THAT A LOT OF PEOPLE WANT A PIECE OF BERNARD MADOFF, WHO FLEECED THOUSANDS OF PEOPLE OUT OF BILLIONS OF DOLLARS IN ONE OF THE LARGEST PONZI SCHEMES IN HISTORY. BUT HOW BADLY DID THEY WANT A PIECE OF MADOFF'S HUNTING GEAR?
One guy paid $11,500 for three wooden duck decoys with a market value of $53 to $80 during an auction to raise money for Madoff's victims. That auction, which raised more than $1 million, also saw one bidder pay $14,500 for Madoff's New York Mets jacket. Nearly all of his possessions—from his clothing to his houses, boats, and cars—sold for much more than valued by the U.S. Marshals Service, which was put in charge of liquidating his assets to compensate those who lost money by investing with him. **Bonus question: How much has the federal government paid to victims of investment fraud?** In 1970, Congress created the Securities Investor Protection Corporation, which paid out $520 million to victims of investment fraud between 1970 and the end of 2008. In 2009, it paid nearly $600 million to Madoff's victims, who lost a total of $19.4 billion.

WHEN IT COMES TO SHOPLIFTING AND EMPLOYEE THEFT, WHICH COUNTRY HAS THE BIGGEST PROBLEM?
If you look at sheer numbers, it's the United States—by far. American retailers lost $42.2 billion in 2009, according to a report based on data from more than 1,000 of the

largest retailers in forty-one countries, including the United States, China, India, Brazil, and Japan. (Other densely populated nations, such as Indonesia, Pakistan, Nigeria, and Russia, were not included in the report, which examined the impact of shoplifting, employee and vendor theft, and administrative errors on retail businesses.) At $9.6 billion, Japan came in a distant second to the United States, followed by the United Kingdom ($7.8 billion) and Germany ($7.1 billion). Of the forty-one countries, retail businesses in Morocco lost the least: $43 million. But if you look at thefts as a percentage of retail sales, India, at 3.2 percent, has the biggest problem, followed by Morocco (1.79), Mexico (1.75), and South Africa (1.72). The United States' rate of theft as a percentage of sales came in at 1.61 percent while Taiwan, at .89 percent, came in last.

A RECENT REPORT OF THE LARGEST RETAILERS IN FORTY-ONE COUNTRIES FOUND THAT 5.8 MILLION PEOPLE WERE APPREHENDED FOR SHOPLIFTING IN 2009. WERE MORE OF THE THIEVES MEN OR WOMEN?

Draw your own conclusions after you read this list of the most common stolen items: clothing, fashion apparel and accessories, auto parts, hardware, building materials, cosmetics, perfume and skin-care products, specialty foods, books, newspapers, stationery, video games, and software.

HOW MUCH DOES IT COST TO REMOVE SNOW IN NEW YORK CITY?

It costs $1 million per inch. The city owns 365 salt spreaders and nearly 2,000 snowplows, and it costs a lot to operate that equipment and pay people to do it. Washington, DC, budgets about $413,000 per inch to clear snow, but the city received four times more snow than it budgeted for during the winter of 2009–10. New York City, which also got clobbered by several winter storms then, was in such desperate straits that it offered to pay residents $12 to $18 per hour to clear snow.

THE BEAR MARKET OF 2007 TO 2009 COST SOME INVESTORS AS MUCH AS 60 PERCENT OF THEIR INVESTMENT PORTFOLIOS BEFORE THE MARKETS BEGAN TO REBOUND. DESPITE THIS, WHAT PERCENTAGE OF RETIREES IN 2009 SAID THEY CONTINUED TO INVEST IN THE STOCK MARKET TO TRY TO ACHIEVE LONG-TERM GAINS?

Nearly three out of four—or 72 percent. Psychologists who study this say Americans have great faith in the long-term benefits of the stock market, and that recessions, even severe ones, do not deter most people from investing. **Bonus question: From 1960 to 2009, which three-day period do Wall Street watchers consider the most volatile?** October 13–15, 2008. October 13 saw the largest percentage gain (11.6 percent) for a day in the Standard & Poor's 500, an index of 500 widely held stocks that represent the U.S. stock market. Just two days later, on October 15, a drop of 9 percent in the S&P 500 made for the second-largest percentage loss in a day during that fifty-year period. **What you can do:** Take some advice from billionaire investor Warren Buffett: (1) buy when everyone else is selling, not when everyone else is buying; (2) be fearful when others are greedy, and be greedy when others are fearful; (3) keep a rainy-day fund for when you need cash; and (4) understand your investments, and don't invest in companies unless you can evaluate their future prospects.

WHEN IT COMES TO SPENDING ON HEALTH CARE AND LIFE EXPECTANCY, THE CITIZENS OF WHICH COUNTRY GET THE MOST BANG FOR THEIR BUCK?

The Japanese. They spend an average of $2,581 per person per year for health care, see their doctors twelve times or more per year, and have an average life expectancy of just under eighty-three, according to a study of thirty developed nations. South Koreans also do well: They spend only $1,688 per year, visit their doctors an average of eight times per year, and have a life expectancy of slightly more than seventy-nine. The United States? Not so well. We spend $7,290 per person—by far the most in the world—and have a life expectancy of about seventy-eight. Mexicans, who have no universal health coverage in their country, spend only $823 per year, and live on average to about seventy-five.

HOW MUCH DOES IT COST TO OPERATE THE AVERAGE GASOLINE-POWERED CAR VERSUS AN ELECTRIC CAR?

It costs about 12 cents per mile for the conventional car compared with 2 cents for the electric one, and the gas-powered car emits about one pound of carbon dioxide per mile compared with .8 pounds for an electric car, which, by the way, gets its power from a coal-burning power plant. So what's stopping us from dumping our cars? The infrastructure is woefully inadequate. Electric cars that go only short distances can be charged at home, but long-distance travel depends on charging stations, and while there are about 117,000 gas stations, there are only about 500 charging stations in the United States, many of which are for business fleets and are not open to the public. But a company called Better Place wants to change that by establishing stations where robots replace depleted batteries with fresh ones. The company hopes to have changing stations operating in Denmark and Israel in 2011 and in Australia, Canada, Hawaii, and California in 2012.

WHAT'S THE MOST ANYONE EVER PAID FOR A WHITE TRUFFLE?

Someone paid $330,000. No, that's not a misprint. In 2007, Macau casino mogul Stanley Ho paid that much for a 3.3-pound Tuscany-grown white truffle, widely considered the highest of high-end delicacies. But that wasn't Ho's first big-ticket purchase: He paid $212,000 for another white truffle in 2008. A group of private equity investors in Hong Kong paid $129,000 for a twenty-seven-ounce white truffle in 2009. A trivial purchase? Maybe, but all of the proceeds of the 2009 sale went to three children's charities.

WHAT'S THE MOST ANYONE EVER PAID FOR LUNCH?

In 2010, $2,626,311. An anonymous bidder paid that to have lunch with billionaire investor Warren Buffett. The money went to the Glide Foundation, which serves the homeless in San Francisco. The $2.6-million bid was up from $1.68 million in 2009—during the worst of the recession—and $2.1 million in 2008. That year a Chinese businessman, Zhao Danyang, the highest bidder, managed to make about $14 million when all was said and done. Zhao leaked to the media the news that he planned to feed Buffet a stock tip: Buy WuMart, a Chinese retailer Zhao thinks will become the next Walmart. That news forced WuMart stock up 25 percent. Zhao's holdings in the company increased by $16 million—a good return on his $2.1-million investment.

HOW ABOUT A CHAIR?

The most anyone ever paid for a chair was $28.3 million. At an auction in Paris in 2009, someone paid that much for a chair made around 1918 by Irish artist Eileen Gray, who mostly lived in Paris. The leather and wooden armchair—part of the estate of fashion designer Yves Saint Laurent and his partner—sold for ten times its auction estimate. To put this in perspective, its sale price equaled the amount paid in 2010 for a 1936 Bugatti Type 57SC Atlantic coupe, which won some of the most prestigious car show prizes. At the auction where the chair was sold, Christie's, the auction house, sold catalogs for that auction for $400—each.

A TRIO OF INVESTORS IN 2009 PAID $1.2 MILLION FOR A THREE-YEAR-OLD COW FROM CANADA NAMED MISSY. WHY IN THE WORLD WOULD ANYONE DO THAT?

Because Missy, short for Eastside Lewisdale Gold Missy, is considered a nearly perfect cow. How do we count the ways? The wide space between her front legs is a sign of a large chest cavity and a healthy heart. Her milk is loaded with protein and makes lots of cheese. The ligaments that support her udder are strong, keeping it farther from the ground and making it less likely that she'll suffer from mammary gland infections. The investors plan to breed Missy and expect that in about seven years, as many as seventy-five cattle will have her genes. They especially hope for male offspring, whose sperm will bring a high price. The $1.2-million cost also includes the rights to sell embryos.

IF MONEY WERE NO OBJECT, WHAT'S ABOUT THE MOST YOU COULD PAY FOR A NEW WATCH?
A watch manufacturer named Richard Mille is selling its Caliber RM020 pocket watch for $450,000. It comes in titanium, 18-karat white or red gold. This is pocket change compared to a pocket watch that sold at auction in 1999 for $11,002,500. The one-pound and three-ounce, twenty-four-function watch—often referred to as the Mona Lisa of watches—was made by Patek Philippe in about 1930.

HOW MUCH WILL SOME PEOPLE PAY FOR A FISH?
A Tokyo restaurant paid $219,755—a record—for a Japanese bluefin tuna that weighed 445.33 pounds, or $493.46 per pound. Japanese restaurants that spend six figures on bluefin tuna will charge $22 or more for a sliver of the fish, which, if prepared properly, will melt in your mouth and be gone before you know it. But these high prices for bluefin may be a thing of the past. The Japanese, who have a long reputation for eating seafood, are eating less of it these days. Monthly household spending on seafood has dipped by 23 percent since 2000.

THE PRICIEST HOTEL ROOM IN THE WORLD?
The Hugh Hefner Sky Villa in the Palms Casino Resort in Las Vegas goes for $40,000 a night—about $6,000 less than the annual median household income in the United

States. The suite, which comes, of course, with a rotating bed and a twelve-person whirl-pool, is only paid for half the nights. The other nights it is given to high rollers. The Ty Warner Penthouse at the Four Seasons New York, which is never discounted, costs $35,000 a night. The suite is decorated with a $120,000 chandelier—no, you can't take it home with you—a waterfall, and a bedspread made of handmade Venetian silk, and you get twenty-four-hour butler service and views of the Chrysler Building, Empire State Building, and the Statue of Liberty.

YOU'RE A TREE HUGGER AND YOU HAVE MORE MONEY THAN MOST OF US. WHAT CAN YOU DO WITH YOUR MONEY AROUND CHRISTMASTIME?

You can *rent* a Christmas tree. That's right: If you live in Los Angeles or Portland or a few other parts of the country, you can rent a short pine tree—complete with an intact root ball packed in a pot—to serve as your Christmas tree for two or three weeks. The small-est trees, those that are two or three feet tall, rent for $50—less than what a lot of people pay for a six-foot-tall live tree. The largest ones rent for nearly $200. After Christmas, the trees go back to the nurseries from which they came. **Bonus question #1: What percentage of Americans choose real trees?** Seventy percent buy real trees, 16 percent display an artificial tree, 9 percent display both, and 5 percent have neither. **Bonus question #2: Where are 85 percent of all artificial Christmas trees made?** China, of course. **What you can do:** Chances are you don't live in a city where you can rent a Christmas tree, but consider buying an artificial tree. The best sales occur right after Christmas.

HOW MUCH MONEY DO YOU HAVE TO MAKE TO INCREASE YOUR CHANCES THAT THE IRS WILL AUDIT YOU?

You have to make at least $200,000. Make less than that, and you have a 1 percent chance of being audited. Make more, and your chances increase to 3 percent. Those who earn $1 million or more have more than a 6 percent chance of being audited. From 2008 to 2009 the number of audits increased by 11 percent for those who earned between $200,000 and just short of $1 million and by 30 percent for those who earned $1 million or more. **Bonus question: What's the median net worth of the top 10 percent of American households?** It's $1.9 million.

HOW RARE IS IT TO BE A BILLIONAIRE IN THE UNITED STATES?

Rare, but not as rare as you might think. Depending on the whims of the stock market and the economy, there are between 305 and 310 Americans worth at least $1.4 billion. And there are 309 million Americans. So one out of every 1 million Americans is worth at least $1.4 billion. **How about millionaires?** About 3 million Americans are millionaires—twice as many as live in Japan and more than three times as many who live in Germany, the countries with the second and third most millionaires. There are about 10 million millionaires in the world. **Bonus question: Who was the first corporate CEO to be paid at least $1 million for one year's work?** In 1929, Eugene Grace, president of Bethlehem Steel, earned $1.62 million—about $21 million in 2010 dollars.

SPEAKING OF MILLIONAIRES, FOOTBALL COACH CHARLIE WEIS, WHO WAS CALLED AN OFFENSIVE MASTERMIND WHEN HE WORKED WITH PROFESSIONAL ATHLETES, BOMBED OUT AFTER FIVE SEASONS AT NOTRE DAME, WHICH PAID HIM $36 MILLION. OF THAT, NOTRE DAME PAID HIM $18 MILLION TO LEAVE BEFORE HIS CONTRACT ENDED. WHAT COULD NOTRE DAME HAVE BOUGHT FOR $36 MILLION?

It could have used that money to pay a student custodian to work 4,931,507 hours. Or it could have bought 3,603,604 Fighting Irish "Defend Our Honor" football T-shirts or 422,287 copies of an accounting textbook. Or it could have awarded 936 full-tuition scholarships or built two new 68,000-square-foot dormitories.

AS ONE OF THE WORLD'S LARGEST EXPORTERS AND IMPORTERS, CHINA CERTAINLY HAS EMBRACED CAPITALISM, NO?

Yes, but consider this: Of the 3,220 Chinese people who are worth at least 100 million yuan ($14.6 million)—a common benchmark to identify that nation's superrich—91 percent are the children of senior Communist Party officials. China scholars say that shows that the party has more to do with who becomes wealthy than does the momentum of capitalism.

THE MAFIA IS INTO DVD PIRACY IN A BIG WAY. WHY?

Money, you knucklehead! Mobsters who control the entire pirated DVD supply chain in their regions reap markups of 1,150 percent—way more than for drugs—and they can expect a relative slap on the wrist if they're caught. According to one estimate, the DVD black market costs governments $1 billion in tax revenue and workers $5.5 billion in lost earnings.

TIPPING IS MORE OF AN EXPECTED PRACTICE IN U.S. RESTAURANTS THAN IT IS JUST ABOUT ANYWHERE ELSE IN THE WORLD. HOW MUCH TIP MONEY DO AMERICAN WAITERS AND WAITRESSES MAKE PER YEAR?

The United States' 2.6 million waiters make $42 billion in tips per year, or an average per waiter of $16,153.85, which comes in handy given that some earn as little as $2.50 an hour. However, the average is skewed. Servers who make less than minimum wage tend to make much less in tips than the average. **What you can do:** Waiters say they expect tips of 20 percent to 25 percent for excellent service, 15 percent to 20 percent for good service, and 10 percent to 15 percent for poor or fair service. Waiters would rather receive no tip than a few pennies. If they receive no tip, they figure there's a chance the diner liked the service but just forgot to leave a tip. If they receive a few pennies, they know the diner thought the service was dreadful.

IF GASOLINE PRICES DROP 10 CENTS PER GALLON, HOW MUCH MONEY DOES THAT PUT IN DRIVERS' POCKETS NATIONWIDE?

It awards them $12 billion. It pays to walk or bike more and drive less. When we drive less, gas prices come down, plus we exercise more and save money. **Bonus question: Which states have the highest and lowest state gasoline taxes?** At 60.9 cents per gallon, New York has the highest tax, followed by California (58.3), Washington (55.9), and Connecticut (54.8). The lowest? Alaska, at 18.4 cents per gallon, then Georgia (30.8), Wyoming (32.4), and Delaware (32.9). The average gas tax of all the states: 45.6 cents.

WHERE IS THE MOST VALUABLE VACANT LOT IN THE WORLD?

The corner of Park Avenue and Fifty-seventh Street in Midtown Manhattan. The lot, adorned with rubble, litter, and tall weeds, sold in 2010 for $305 million—a steal when you consider the previous owner paid $418 million for it, then borrowed against it so that it was actually worth $543 million. The lot is the site of the former Drake Hotel, which was built in 1926 and demolished in 2007 by developer Harry Macklowe, who intended to build an office tower there. Macklowe's business tanked when the real estate bubble began to burst in 2008. He partnered with a private-equity firm in 2010 to try to regain control of the lot from the bank that foreclosed on it but ended up selling it to a California-based investment firm.

WHAT'S THE MOST EXTREME EXAMPLE OF RENT-CONTROLLED APARTMENTS IN THE WORLD?

At the Fuggerei, in Augsburg, Germany, the *annual* rent is one Rhein guilder—the equivalent of 88 (euro) cents, or about $1.23—the same as in 1520, when sixteenth-century financier Jakob Fugger built the Roman Catholic housing settlement for the poor. The catch: Residents must pray daily for Fugger and his descendants to enter heaven. **Bonus question: New York City is known for its many rent-controlled apartments. There are about 850,000** of them. **What's the least anyone is paying there?** Someone is paying $58 a month to live in Little Italy, and another renter is paying $60 to live in an apartment on the Lower East Side.

WHAT IS BELIEVED TO BE THE BIGGEST PRICE CUT FOR A SINGLE-FAMILY HOUSE IN THE UNITED STATES?

The biggest price cut is $52 million. Virginia philanthropist Patricia Kluge cut the price of her 300-acre estate from $100 million to $48 million in late 2009. The forty-five-room, 23,500-square-foot house with eight bedrooms and thirteen bathrooms is the highlight of the estate, but the premises also include a theater, spa, pool, log cabin, greenhouse, and several cottages for staff. **The second-biggest price cut:** $50 million. The asking price for Dunnellen Hall, the 20,000-square-foot brick mansion once owned by hotel heiress Leona Helmsley, went from $125 million to $75 million in April 2009. That house, in Greenwich, Connecticut, has two pools, thirteen bedrooms—six for servants—and views of the Long Island Sound. **Bonus question: What's the highest-ever median sales price for new houses sold in the United States, and when was that record achieved?** It was $254,000, in March 2007.

WHICH STATE SAW THE HIGHEST INCREASES IN HOME PRICES FROM THE START OF 2005 TO THE END OF 2009, A PERIOD WHEN THE HOUSING BUBBLE BURST AND HAD YET TO RECOVER?

Wyoming. Housing prices there jumped 27 percent. Other states that did well during this glum period for real estate include Montana and Nevada (both 23 percent), Louisiana (21.5 percent), New Mexico (21 percent), and Utah (20 percent). The states where you didn't want to own a house from 2005 through 2009? Nevada, which saw a 40 percent price decline, followed by California (27 percent), Michigan (23 percent), and Florida (19 percent). Housing prices in Nevada rose 37 percent, the lowest increase between 1991 and 2009, while prices soared by 234 percent in Washington, DC, during that period.

WHEN WILL PAINTING YOUR WALLS BRIGHT PINK COST YOU $3,500?

When you put your house up for sale. A team of scientists who studied what people look at when they look at real estate ads on the Internet found that those who viewed a house with a room painted bright pink valued the house $3,500 less than an identical house without a bright pink room. The study also found that people who saw power lines in a photo valued it at $13,500 less than houses advertised without photos of power lines. The researchers said their study—which included forty-seven people, twenty of whom were house shoppers—is the first to use ocular tracking to determine preferences of those house hunting on the Internet. "We know exactly where you're looking," one researcher said. "We know how long you're focusing on it—whether you're reading or you're just glancing." **What you can do:** If you're prepping your house for sale, real estate agents urge you to purge the clutter and paint your walls neutral colors. Why? You want to make it easy for prospective buyers to picture themselves in the house you want to sell, and they can't do that as easily if they can't get the turquoise-colored walls out of their minds. If you're a buyer, try to look at the stuff that makes you want to gag. A lot of people can't do that, and they miss out on great deals.

WHO WERE THE MOST UNUSUAL HOME BUYERS TO TAKE ADVANTAGE OF THE $8,000 TAX CREDIT OFFERED BY THE U.S. GOVERNMENT IN 2009 AND 2010 TO EASE THE NATION'S HOUSING SLUMP?

The Internal Revenue Service identified about 75,000 questionable claims. Of those, 582 were made by buyers younger than eighteen, including a few as young as four years old. The government allocated about $15 billion for first-time home buyers, including $4 million to children, who, the government later learned, were ineligible to make those claims. At least fifty-three IRS workers—all adults—also filed claims deemed "illegal or inappropriate."

HOW MANY AMERICANS WORK FULL-TIME YEAR-ROUND AND STILL LIVE BELOW THE POVERTY LEVEL?

There are 2,906,000. Of those, nearly 1.3 million are in their prime wage-earning years—between thirty-five and fifty-four years old.

WHAT PERCENTAGE OF AMERICAN FAMILIES (BY RACE) LIVES BELOW THE POVERTY LEVEL?

People identified themselves: 21.6 percent as black, 18.9 percent as Hispanic, 8 percent as white, and 7.8 percent as Asian. The rest identified themselves as mixed races.

WHAT PERCENTAGE OF AMERICANS SAYS THEY LIVE PAYCHECK TO PAYCHECK? OF THOSE, WHAT PERCENTAGE MAKE MORE THAN $100,000 A YEAR?

Forty-seven percent live paycheck to paycheck, and 21 percent of those workers earn more than $100,000 a year. Given that, it should come as no surprise that 27 percent of American workers have saved less than $1,000 for retirement, and six out of ten workers who are fifty-five or older have retirement nest eggs of less than $100,000. **What you can do:** Financial advisors recommend funneling as much of your income as you can afford into a 401(k) or other tax-free investments, especially if your employer matches some or all of what you contribute.

WHAT PERCENTAGE OF RETIREES MAKES MONTHLY MORTGAGE PAYMENTS?

Fifty-two. Not only has that percentage increased during the past two decades but so has the average amount of each mortgage. In 1992, 17 percent of households ages sixty-five to seventy-four were paying off mortgages, and the average mortgage was about $35,000. Today the 52 percent who are still paying have mortgages of about $85,000. **What you can do:** Live modestly, but don't invest too conservatively. In a recent survey, conservative investors reported a median net worth of $671,000 compared to

$836,000 for retirees who owned different types of financial products. Bottom line: Diversify.

OF THE NEARLY 7 BILLION PEOPLE IN THE WORLD TODAY, ABOUT HOW MANY LIVE ON LESS THAN $1 A DAY?
One billion. And at least 80 percent of the world—or 5.6 billion—lives on less than $10 a day.

WHAT PERCENTAGE OF CHILDREN IN THE UNITED STATES, THE WORLD'S RICHEST NATION, LIVE IN POVERTY?
Nearly 17 percent—or one out of six. Of those, 44 percent live in homes headed by single mothers. Nearly six out of ten live outside major cities and are much more likely to be African American and Latino than white.

WHO PAYS MORE FOR GROCERIES—THE RICH OR THE POOR?
The poor. Poorer urban residents depend more on locally owned stores than do wealthier suburbanites, and those stores typically have fewer goods and charge more for them, partially to make up for theft. The poor pay about 7 percent more than those who shop at chain supermarkets, which sell higher volumes and can afford to offer larger discounts. Some call this a "ghetto tax."

YOU WOULD BE RIGHT TO ASSUME THAT THE UNITED STATES, THE RICHEST COUNTRY IN THE WORLD, HAS THE MOST CARS PER 1,000 PEOPLE. BUT WHICH COUNTRIES HAVE THE NEXT MOST, AND WHICH HAVE THE LEAST?
With 787 motor vehicles per 1,000 people, the United States leads Portugal (765), Luxemburg (756), and Iceland (724). In Nigeria and Cambodia, there is one motor

vehicle for every 1,000 people. **Bonus question: In which country were the most automobiles sold in 2009?** China, where 12.7 million autos were sold. This was also the first year any country sold more autos in one year than did the United States, which sold 10.4 million.

WHO TEND TO MAKE MORE MONEY—MEN WHO THINK WOMEN BELONG AT HOME OR MEN WHO THINK WOMEN BELONG WHEREVER THEY WANT TO BE?

Men who say women should have a traditional role made $8,549 more than other men, according to researchers who analyzed data and interviewed workers. Why? Here are two theories: (1) men with old-fashioned values negotiate salaries more aggressively because they are more likely to be their families' only breadwinners, while other men consider aggressive negotiation to be unattractive, alpha-male behavior; and (2) employers unconsciously pay less to men who think everyone, women included, should be treated equally. The researchers say no one should interpret their findings as a reason to raise boys to be chauvinists.

IF YOU'RE TALLER THAN THE GUY IN THE CUBICLE NEXT TO YOU, DO YOU PROBABLY MAKE MORE OR LESS THAN HIM?

Probably more, according to a study of British workers. The economists who reached this conclusion found that each additional inch equals an average increase in wages of 1.5 percent to 1.8 percent. Why? Here are the two most popular theories: Tall people are believed to be tall in part because their parents gave them advantages—for example, a good diet, vitamins, and proper health care—that allowed them to reach their physical potential, and so they are more likely to reach their cognitive potential as adults. The other theory has even more to do with perception: Tall people are believed to be more qualified for a high-skilled job—and worthy of more money—by virtue of their physical status. **What you can do:** If you're tall, be grateful. If you're short, just work hard and accept the fact that life ain't fair.

MEN MAKE MORE MONEY THAN WOMEN, BUT WHO HAS MORE PURCHASING POWER?

Women do. Men earn $23.4 trillion annually worldwide, compared with $10.5 trillion for women, but women control $12 trillion of the $18.4 trillion in annual consumer spending, according to a survey of more than 12,000 women in twenty-two countries. Women are replacing men in the workplace, and earnings and spending power for women are expected to grow much faster than for men during the next five years.

HOW MUCH DOES IT COST TO SHIP CORN TO AFRICA RATHER THAN JUST GIVE SEED AND FERTILIZER TO AFRICAN FARMERS?

It costs the United States about $812 to buy a ton of corn, ship it to Africa, and distribute it. It would cost $135 to give African farmers the seed and fertilizer and teach them the best way to grow the corn.

HOW LONG DOES IT TAKE THE COST OF A PUBLIC COLLEGE EDUCATION TO CATCH UP WITH THE COST OF A PRIVATE COLLEGE EDUCATION?

About twenty-two years. During the 1987–88 school year, tuition and fees at an average private university cost $7,048. During the 2009–10 school year, tuition and fees at an average public university cost $7,020. If you factor in room and board, public colleges cost an average of $15,213 for the 2009–10 school year—the result of 6.2 percent increases during the past twenty years. If college costs increased by 2.8 percent—the annual inflation rate during the past twenty years—a year of tuition, fees, and room and board at a public college would have cost $7,889 during the 2009–10 school year. **What you can do:** If you have a child and want to send him to college, financial advisors say it's never too early to start saving. Consider state-sponsored savings plans, but read the fine print; some are not guaranteed, and many have restrictions.

WHICH COLLEGE STUDENTS MAKE THE MOST MONEY IN THEIR FIRST JOBS?

Petroleum engineer majors with job offers in 2010 made an annual salary of $86,220. Other types of engineering majors also pay recent grads well. **Bonus question: A college degree is a good thing for a lot of people to have, but is it worth $800,000 or $1 million in increased life-time earnings for the recipient, as is so often quoted?** Not usually. The $800,000 figure was widely used by the College Board, the Census Bureau, and others, but a growing number of economists say the income gap between high school and college graduates is much smaller—more reasonably between $275,000 and $450,000 during a lifetime of working. The inflated figure, which the College Board no longer touts, didn't take into account a number of factors, including rising tuition costs. While the high school graduate is working and earning a salary, his college student peer is earning no salary and ratcheting up debt—and interest on that debt. What's more, some college graduates never land jobs that pay better than the jobs found by high school graduates.

HOW MUCH MONEY DO U.S. BUSINESSES LOSE DURING THE FIRST WEEK OF THE NCAA BASKETBALL TOURNAMENT BECAUSE THEIR EMPLOYEES SNEAK AWAY TO WATCH THE GAMES OR FOLLOW THEM ON THEIR OFFICE COMPUTERS?

They lose $1.8 billion. Because so many workers play office pools, many people consider it a right to watch the games, even while they should be working. But 33 percent of U.S. employers forbid March Madness office gambling pools, and that tends to cut down on basketball viewing during work hours. **Bonus question: In December 2009 and January 2010, the men's basketball team at the University of Arkansas–Pine Bluff played its first fourteen games as a road team—one of the longest streaks in college basketball history. Why?** Money, of course. The team received $70,000 per game—$980,000 in all—for its efforts from the host schools. The school said the team did so to help financially support the program. After football, basketball is the second-most-expensive sport for a college to field. By the way, Arkansas–Pine Bluff lost its first eleven games, and then won eighteen of its next twenty-two games to earn its first-ever NCAA tournament bid. It lost to Duke University by 29 points in the first round.

Four

BON APPÉTIT

We may not talk about food and drink as much as we talk about money, but we need them more. In this chapter, you'll find out how seaweed ends up in your toothpaste, how seriously you should take the ratings you see on wine bottles, and how much it would cost to make school lunches healthy. Which countries eat the least meat? Why does the world need more apple-ring acacia trees? And we'll answer this and other burning questions: Are Filet-O-Fish sandwiches really made of fish?

WHICH BEVERAGE IS MOST ENVIRONMENTALLY FRIENDLY—MILK, BEER, TEA, WINE OR COFFEE?
Tea. It takes nine gallons of water to make a cup of tea, and that includes the water to grow the plants and process the leaves. Compare that to beer (20 gallons), wine (32 gallons), coffee (37 gallons), and milk (53 gallons). Coffee and tea actually require

about the same amount of water to grow the plants, but tea has a higher yield per acre, so it's more environmentally friendly. Milk ranks highest on this list because cows require so much water. A cow that lives three years—the average from birth to market—requires about 816,600 so-called virtual gallons of water. Of that, 808,400 are for irrigating the fields of feed and hay it eats, 6,300 are for drinking, and 1,900 are for cleaning its stables.

EVERYONE SAYS COMPARING APPLES AND ORANGES IS THE WRONG THING TO DO, BUT WHICH ONE IS MORE NUTRITIOUS?

Oranges—barely. An apple has fewer calories (57) than an orange (85) and less sugar (11.3 grams vs. 16.8 grams), but an orange has more fiber (4.3 grams) than an apple (2.6 grams) and way more vitamin C (96 milligrams vs. 5 milligrams for an apple). Oranges also show up more often on lists of so-called superfoods—foods that dieticians and nutritionists say are most nutritious. **What you can do:** Eat apples and oranges, but don't forget these other fruits, which routinely make the lists of superfoods: blueberries, tomatoes, kiwis, and apricots.

HOW MUCH MORE WOULD A SCHOOL LUNCH COST IF THE HOT DOGS, PIZZA, FRENCH FRIES AND OTHER FAST FOOD FROM CAFETERIAS WERE REPLACED WITH FRESHLY PREPARED FOOD?

At least $1 per lunch per day. With about 50 million children in public elementary, middle, and high schools in the United States and a 180-day school year, it would cost at least $9 billion a year to give public school students freshly prepared food. That sounds like a lot of money—and it is—but it's less than a third of what the United States was paying per month to fund the Iraq War. **Bonus question: What percentage of public schools in the United States doesn't serve either fresh fruit or raw vegetables daily?** About forty. **What you can do:** The U.S. Department of Agriculture says it's possible to get your five daily servings of fruits or vegetables for about $1, so if your child must buy that hot dog in the cafeteria, pack something healthy to go along with it—and then pray that he actually eats it.

WHAT ARE THE ELEVEN HEALTHIEST FOODS THAT ARE EASY TO FIND BUT ONLY OCCASIONALLY MAKE THEIR WAY INTO GROCERY CARTS?

In no particular order: beets (great source of folate), cabbage (loaded with nutrients, at least one of which boosts cancer-fighting enzymes), Swiss chard (packed with nutrients), cinnamon (may help control blood sugar and cholesterol), pomegranate juice (may lower blood pressure and loaded with antioxidants), prunes (lots of antioxidants), pumpkin seeds (contain magnesium, which in high levels may lower risk for early death), sardines (high in omega-3's and loaded with calcium and iron, magnesium, phosphorus, potassium, zinc, copper, and manganese as well as a full complement of B vitamins), turmeric (a spice that may have anti-inflammatory and anticancer properties), frozen blueberries (packed with nutrients), and canned pumpkin (high in fiber and vitamin A and low in calories).

IN WHICH COUNTRIES ARE YOU LEAST AND MOST LIKELY TO FIND VEGETARIANS?

At 321.7 pounds per person per year, citizens of Denmark eat the most meat, followed by New Zealand (313.3), Luxembourg (312.4), Cyprus (289.5), and the United States (275.1). At 6.6 pounds per person per year, Bhutan—a tiny, landlocked country between India and China—eats the least. Other countries with little meat consumption include Bangladesh (6.8 pounds), Burundi (7.7), Rwanda (9.7), and the Democratic Republic of Congo (10.6). This has more to do with what people in these poor nations can afford rather than what they choose to eat. In sheer numbers, Americans eat the most beef and chicken and Chinese the most pork.

BON APPÉTIT

AMERICANS LOVE THEIR BURGERS, BACON, AND FRIED CHICKEN. ABOUT HOW MANY ANIMALS HAVE TO GIVE THEIR LIVES EACH YEAR TO SATISFY OUR APPETITES?

About 35 million cows, more than 110 million pigs, and 9 billion chickens and turkeys. As many as 450 billion chickens live in the United States at any one time, many of which are crowded in warehouses, never see sunlight, and can hardly stand on their own because they're bred to be so top-heavy.

IS McDONALD'S FILET-O-FISH SANDWICH REALLY MADE WITH FISH?

Yes. Most of the sandwiches start with a silvery fish called hoki, or whiptail, which come from the waters off New Zealand. McDonald's, which uses between 10 million and 15 million pounds of hoki per year, also uses other whitefish, including pollock. Conservationists worry that the demand for cheap whitefish is endangering hoki—a concern that has caused New Zealand to reduce the annual allowable catch from 275,000 tons to 100,000 tons. McDonald's, like other restaurant chains, has had to compensate by using other whitefish.

BEACHGOERS TEND TO REVILE SEAWEED, BUT HOW IS IT UNDERRATED?

There happens to be a $14 billion global market for seaweed, which is an ingredient in a diverse group of products, including toothpaste, cosmetics, and chicken patties. In fact, seaweed has been used for centuries to add texture in foods, especially in Asia, but demand increased dramatically in the 1960s, when some companies began using it to provide texture to ice cream and other things.

WHAT'S THE LEAST HEALTHY BEVERAGE YOU CAN DRINK?

No, it's not grain alcohol. Try—or better yet, don't try—Baskin-Robbins' Large Chocolate Oreo Shake, which contains 2,600 calories, 135 grams of fat (59 grams of saturated fat and 2.5 grams of trans fat), 263 grams of sugar, and 1,700 milligrams of sodium. *Men's Health* magazine, which called it the unhealthiest drink in America, has this to say about it: "Is this the worst drink on the planet? All signs point to yes. First off, it has an ingredient list that reads like an organic chemistry final. Those 70-plus ingredients conspire to pack this shake with more sugar than 29 Fudgsicles, as much fat as a stick and a half of butter and more calories than 48 actual Oreos. Oh, it also has three days' worth of saturated fat and, most bizarre of all, as much salt as you'll find in nine bags of Lay's Classic potato chips. Need more proof? Let's hope not." **What you can do:** It's obvious: Stay away from that heart-attack-waiting-to-happen. What to drink? Doctors say water is the healthiest beverage, followed by milk. How about fruit juices? A growing number of doctors pooh-pooh them, especially for overweight children, because many of them contain a lot of sugar.

HOW MUCH SODA DO AMERICANS DRINK PER YEAR?

Fifty gallons per person. Those who think that's too much point out that sugared beverages are the top source of calories for Americans—7 percent for the average person and 10 percent for children—and that heavy soda consumption contributes to childhood obesity. Because of that, there has been much talk of taxing soda. Taxes on sodas can generate an enormous amount of money and lead to a decrease in soda consumption. Arkansas, Tennessee, Virginia, Washington, and West Virginia have soda taxes, as does Chicago. And other cities and states are considering them. A proposal to place a 3-cent federal tax on each twelve-ounce can of soda would have generated about $5 billion a year, but it was defeated in 2009. If it were enacted, nutrition consultants predicted soda consumption would have dipped from 50 gallons per person per year to 38.5 gallons. Lobbyists are working furiously to defeat proposed soda taxes throughout the nation. The American Beverage Association, which represents PepsiCo, Inc. and Coca-Cola

Company, among others, spent $19 million on lobbying in 2009—$18.3 more than in 2008. Canada Dry offered Philadelphia $10 million as a goodwill gesture as the city mulled a soda tax in 2010. (Philadelphia killed the tax and turned down the money.) Also in 2010, PepsiCo gave the Yale School of Medicine $250,000 to create a research fellowship to study obesity and nutrition. **What you can do:** If you're hooked on soda, most dieticians say it's unrealistic to think you can stop drinking it cold turkey. Cut your consumption in half. If you drink two cans of soda per day, opt for one can of soda and drink a glass of water instead of that second soda. Feel bad for Coke and Pepsi? You can buy bottled water from Coke (Dasani) and Pepsi (Aquafina), but keep in mind that they're just purified tap water.

ONCE AND FOR ALL, COFFEE . . . GOOD OR BAD?

Both. Plenty of recent studies have trumpeted coffee's healing powers, making it seem like a staple of any healthy diet, but it also can do more harm than just staining your teeth. First, the pros: It lowers the risk of developing type-2 diabetes, gallstones, stroke, and cancer of the colon, throat, and mouth. It doesn't raise the risk of heart disease, as once thought. It may help battle Alzheimer's disease, and it boosts energy and curbs depression. The downside: It can raise the risk of miscarriage and low-birth-weight babies and cause anxiety, upset stomach, and caffeine-withdrawal symptoms, including headaches, fatigue, and hyperactivity. It also lowers bone density, and it raises the level of bad cholesterol and blood pressure as well as blood sugar in diabetes sufferers. **What you can do:** If you like coffee, drink it in moderation—a cup or two per day.

WE'VE ALSO HEARD A LOT ABOUT THE BENEFITS OF QUAFFING WINE IN MODERATION, BUT WHY ARE SOME DOCTORS SAYING THAT'S NOT ALWAYS A GOOD IDEA?

Women who once suffered from breast cancer may be more likely to have it recur if they drink even a few glasses of wine per week, according to a study that tracked the eating and drinking habits of 1,897 women who were diagnosed with early-stage breast cancer from 1997 to 2000. Half of the women said they drank alcohol, mostly wine. After following up for eight years, the researchers found that the alcohol drinkers—even those who drank moderately—were 34 percent more likely to suffer a recurrence of the disease than those who drank very little alcohol or none at all. The theory: Alcohol increases levels of estrogen—the main sex hormone in women—and that may increase the chances of recurrence.

BUT IF YOU DON'T HAVE A HISTORY OF BREAST CANCER, THERE'S NOTHING WRONG WITH DRINKING ONE GLASS OF WINE PER DAY, RIGHT?

Not when you're pregnant. A study of 289 eight-year-olds in Finland found that children whose mothers drank the equivalent of one glass of wine per day while they were in the womb were two and a half times as likely to sleep fewer than 7.7 hours per night as children whose mothers didn't drink during pregnancy. A child's sleep was not affected when mothers smoked during pregnancy. **What you can do:** The vast majority of doctors urge pregnant women to cut down on alcohol, to, say, no more than a few drinks per week, if that.

HOW SERIOUSLY SHOULD YOU TAKE THE RATINGS YOU SEE ON WINE BOTTLES?

Not very, according to numerous studies. One study, the most comprehensive, tested about 260 judges who work the California State Fair Commercial Wine Competition, the oldest and most prestigious in North America. The judges tasted each wine three times without knowing what they were drinking. On average, a judge's score varied by four points. That may sound consistent, but it means, for example, a wine could be awarded 91 points on the first tasting, 87 on the second, and 95 on the third. Only one judge out of ten varied his scores by 2 points. Nine out of nine were less consistent than that. The study shows that wine judging is, in fact, subjective and can greatly affect sales because many consumers pay close attention to ratings. **What you can do:** Confused about wine? The vast majority of wineshop workers will gladly advise you on what to buy if you tell them how much you'd like to spend. There's more good inexpensive wine available than ever before.

EVERYONE KNOWS BREAST MILK IS THE BEST THING YOU CAN GIVE A NEWBORN. IF YOU'RE A BABY BORN TO A TEENAGE MOTHER, ARE YOU MORE LIKELY TO RECEIVE BREAST MILK IF YOUR MOTHER IS WHITE, BLACK, OR MEXICAN AMERICAN?

Mexican American—and it's not even close. Sixty-six percent of Mexican American teen mothers gave their children breast milk at least once compared with 40 percent of white teen mothers and 30 percent of black teen mothers, according to a recent study. The same holds true for mothers between the ages of twenty and twenty-nine. For mothers between thirty and thirty-nine, 77 percent of white women gave their babies breast milk at least once, just ahead of Mexican American women (76 percent), and way ahead of black women (56 percent). **What you can do:** Doctors almost unanimously encourage mothers to breast-feed.

HOW MANY POPPY SEED BAGELS COULD YOU MAKE IF AFGHANISTAN SET ASIDE ITS ENTIRE ANNUAL CROP FOR THAT INNOCENT PURPOSE?

Three hundred and fifty-seven billion. Other leading producers of poppy seeds include the Czech Republic, Turkey, France, Hungary, Germany, Israel, and Austria.

NEED ANOTHER REASON TO LIKE CHOCOLATE?

A new study says it may be good for the heart. Spanish researchers gave chocolate milk—skim milk with cocoa powder—to twenty-one people with a high risk of heart disease twice a day for four weeks and plain skim milk to twenty-one others who were also at risk for heart disease. The researchers found that the chocolate milk helped reduce or prevent fat from blocking the arteries. The chocolate milk drinkers, who had an average age of seventy, also ended up with higher levels of good cholesterol.

YEAH, BUT CHOCOLATE CAN MAKE YOU FAT, AND WHAT ELSE CAN IT MAKE YOU?

Depressed. A study of 931 adults who weren't taking antidepressants screened the participants for signs of depression and found that people who weren't depressed ate an average of 5.4 servings of chocolate per month while people who were "possibly depressed" ate 8.4 servings per month, and those who were very likely to suffer from depression ate an average of 11.8 servings per month. The researchers looked at other foods, such as fruits and vegetables and fish, and identified no link between them and depression. However, the researchers concede they don't know for sure whether the people in the study were already depressed and turned to chocolate as a comfort food or whether the chocolate they ate made them more depressed.

RICE IS ARGUABLY THE MOST IMPORTANT FOOD IN THE WORLD, WITH GLOBAL SHORTAGES TRANSLATING TO LIFE-AND-DEATH SITUATIONS FOR TENS OF MILLIONS OF PEOPLE. IS ANYTHING BEING DONE TO ENSURE THE WORLD SUPPLY OF IT?

Yes. A genetically enhanced version, which hit the markets in Southeast Asia in 2009, survives for as long as eighteen days underwater, compared with four days for traditional varieties. Surviving underwater is a big deal in Southeast Asia, much of which is vulnerable to flooding from typhoons and other rain-drenching storms. A cyclone in 2007, for example, wiped out 1.25 million tons of rice in Bangladesh.

THE 2010 HEALTH CARE BILL REQUIRED RESTAURANT CHAINS TO LIST THE CALORIES FOR FOOD. HOW MUCH DO THOSE MENUS INFLUENCE WHAT DINERS ORDER?

Not much, according to recent studies. In one study, researchers interviewed more than 20,000 customers at thirteen restaurant chains, and 56 percent said they noticed the calorie information, but only about a quarter of those who noticed it said they made choices based on that information. The group that made choices based on calories bought meals with, on average, 106 fewer calories, but that group made up only about 15 percent of the 20,000 or so customers who were interviewed.

WHEN IT COMES TO FIGURING OUT HOW MANY CALORIES ARE IN FOOD, ARE AMERICANS PRETTY GOOD GUESSERS?

Uh, not exactly. One study found that restaurant diners underestimated the number of calories in an order of cheese fries with ranch dressing by an average of 2,141 calories, chicken fajitas by 956 calories, fettuccine Alfredo by 796 calories, chef's salad by 478 calories, and a burger and fries by 463 calories. **But it's not all bad news:** The diners underestimated the number of calories in turkey by only 12 and overestimated the number of calories in pot roast by 43.

HOW MUCH SWINE WASTE DOES SMITHFIELD FOODS, THE WORLD'S LARGEST PORK PRODUCER, FLUSH INTO GIANT LAGOONS?

Smithfield Foods has become so large that the amount of waste they generate equals the amount produced by everyone who lives in California and Texas combined. The good news is the waste is eaten by bacteria. The bad news is that it doesn't always stay in those lagoons, and can pollute nearby rivers and streams by, among other things, sucking out the oxygen and suffocating fish. In 1995, an eight-acre holding pond operated by a different pork producer failed, allowing 25 million gallons of waste into the New River in North Carolina.

WHY DO FARMERS IN WESTERN AFRICA LOVE THE APPLE-RING ACACIA TREE?

The tree sheds its leaves at the *start* of the growing season rather than at the end, and those leaves are especially rich in nitrogen, so they do a great job of fertilizing the soil after they decay. How great? Researchers in Zambia and Malawi recently found that maize near the trees' canopies increased crop yield by about 300 percent. The agriculture departments in those countries want to use the trees to double maize production, so they recommend farmers plant them in their fields.

Five

MONKEY STALKERS, GIANT DUST CLOUDS AND CHICKEN FEATHERS

Monkey stalkers, giant dust clouds, and chicken feathers can only be about one thing—recent discoveries in science. In this chapter, you'll learn why Neanderthals were cuter than we give them credit for, why dreams say more about our bodies than our minds, and why Russian space scientists are so worried about a particular asteroid—but American scientists are not. The chapter also reveals the worst thing that can happen to Earth, the happiest job in science, and biologists' latest discoveries about bees, pigs, and toucans. You'll also find out what the *E. coli* bacterium, chicken feathers, and coffee grounds have in common.

WHAT ARE SOME OF THE STRANGEST AND WORST JOBS IN SCIENCE?

Here are seven:

- A German researcher watches monkeys have sex in Gibraltar, as does a Canadian biologist in Japan. The Canadian discovered that female Japanese macaques prefer other females 92 percent of the time.

- An American researcher collects leeches throughout the world by wading into swamps and letting them suck his blood. After he peels them off, he studies them to understand them better before handing them over to be used in reconstructive surgery and other scientific pursuits.

- Six pilots and scientists agreed to be locked in a series of metal tubes in Moscow and videotaped by eighteen cameras for 520 days to simulate a round-trip voyage to Mars.

- Italian scientists, wearing scuba gear, dive into giant masses of mucus in the Mediterranean Sea to try to determine why plankton are producing so much of it.

- A California researcher measures how much mucus and saliva are released when someone sneezes in someone else's face.

- American scientists collect and save foul odors so that one day they can figure out how to identify certain cancers that emit bad smells.

- Any number of biologists and zoologists cut open beached whales and other marine mammals to try to determine how they died. That never smells good, but scientists who make the wrong cuts can release nauseous gases that can linger on their clothes and skin for weeks.

THE HAPPIEST JOB IN SCIENCE?

An English neuroscientist set out to compare the laughter of baby humans and baby apes when they're tickled. She recorded the laughter of her colleagues' babies, and then traveled the world to record the laughter of baby chimps, gorillas, and bonobos. In most cases, the apes' caregivers did the tickling because, like humans, ape babies don't like to be tickled by strangers. The neuroscientist's conclusion? Laughter from tickling started about 10 million to 16 million years ago. Guess someone needed to discover that. **Bonus question: What are the most ticklish areas of the body?** Underarms, waist, ribs, feet, knees, throat, neck, and palms. **What you can do:** Tickling is a way to show affection and get a positive response—i.e., laughter—but most people past the age of forty never do it, and social scientists say that's a bad thing. We need to laugh more, they say, and even wanting to laugh more is a good thing. Even if you're having a fight with your partner, try tickling him or her instead of walking out of the room. Even an angry partner may appreciate what you're trying to do.

RUSSIA'S TOP SPACE RESEARCHERS ARE VERY WORRIED ABOUT 99942 APOPHIS, AN ASTEROID THAT WILL PASS RELATIVELY NEAR EARTH STARTING IN 2029. WHAT DO THEY WANT TO DO ABOUT IT, AND WHY DO MOST AMERICAN SCIENTISTS THINK THAT'S A WASTE OF TIME?

Russians have been meeting to talk about either creating a missile to strike the 1,000-foot-long asteroid or building a spacecraft that would attach itself to the asteroid and direct it away from Earth. While some Russian scientists think there's a very real possibility that it will hit Earth, most American researchers are puzzled by Russia's reaction to the asteroid, which NASA discovered in 2004. NASA believes that on the asteroid's first approach, in 2029, it should remain 18,300 miles away. There's a 1 in 250,000 chance it will hit Earth on its second approach, in 2036, and a 1 in 333,000 chance on its third approach, in 2068.

DID YOU HEAR THE ONE ABOUT THE ROBOT AND THE VOLLEYBALL? OR IS IT THE ROBOTIC VOLLEYBALL?

It's a robot that looks like a volleyball that needs air, and it is able to expand and contract its silicone shell, changing shape and causing it to move. The researchers' work is funded by the Defense Department, which wants robots that can fit into small spaces during reconnaissance missions to record information.

WHAT SURPRISING BIT OF NEWS DID THE WORLD LEARN ABOUT NEANDERTHALS IN 2010?

Neanderthals, not known for being a handsome lot, used makeup and wore jewelry, according to researchers who found shells stained with pigment at Neanderthal camps in southeastern Spain. These and other scientists conclude that the ability to make paints proves that Neanderthals were not as dim-witted as previously thought and that the makeup and jewelry proves they valued individuality and cared about their appearance. **Bonus question: If Neanderthals had strong, thick-limbed bodies and evolved to adapt to the cold, why didn't they survive?** Neanderthals, whose remains have been found as far west as Portugal and as far east as central Asia, adapted to handle the cold, but they didn't handle severe fluctuations in the climate very well, and they clashed with Africans who moved into Europe and Asia. Eventually the Africans pushed the Neanderthals into small pockets, restricting their hunting efforts. This hurt them because as they evolved, they developed a need for lots of calories and needed meat to fulfill that need. Anthropologists believe women and children were forced to hunt, a very dangerous and potentially fatal undertaking back then.

WHAT'S THE OLDEST THING ON EARTH, AND WHAT HAS IT TAUGHT US?

Zircons. Scientists who date old things say zircons, tiny crystals embedded in old rocks in western Australia, are the only documented things older than 4 billion years old. Some are as old as 4.4 billion years old. Geologists who study them say the crystals have helped them learn a lot about Earth back then, including shattering a long-held belief that the world was a hot and desolate place. Scientists now say that 4 billion years ago Earth was a place with land and oceans, and it wasn't as hot as once believed because the sun put out 30 percent less energy than it does today. Many Christians don't believe Earth is 4 billion years old, but they find this discovery encouraging. This milder, newly created world more closely matches the description of creation in the Bible.

WHAT'S ABOUT THE WORST THING THAT CAN HAPPEN TO EARTH?

Meteors are small potatoes compared to giant dust clouds on the edge of our galaxy that are so large it would take our solar system about 100,000 years to pass through them. And while the Milky Way was passing through, the clouds would almost entirely block the sun, causing the oceans to freeze and all life to die. **What you can do:** Don't run off and buy insurance just yet. Scientists say we shouldn't expect the dust clouds for about 40 million years.

WHAT WOULD HAPPEN TO EARTH IF THE SUN WENT AWAY FOR GOOD?

Within a week, the average temperature would plummet to just below 0 degrees F, down to minus 100 degrees F a year later. Although much of the oceans would freeze over, the top layer of ice would actually insulate the lower layers of water, preventing the oceans from freezing solid for hundreds of thousands of years.

WHAT'S THE BIGGEST SCIENCE EXPERIMENT EVER?

The Large Hadron Collider, which lies 164 feet to 574 feet under the Franco-Swiss border not far from Geneva, is the world's largest and highest-energy particle accelerator, colliding beams of protons around a seventeen-mile-long racetrack at approximately 99.9999991 percent of the speed of light. Here are some other numbers that help explain why the collider has been called the modern equivalent of the Egyptian pyramids: It took more than 10,000 scientists and engineers from more than one hundred countries fifteen years to build it at a cost of $10 billion and counting. About 4,700 miles of superconducting cable help to power 1,232 thirty-five-ton magnets that steer the protons around the track until they collide. Scientists study the collisions with a pretty lofty goal: to tell mankind a lot of what it doesn't know about the structure of the universe. Shortly after the collider was turned on in September 2008, thousands of improperly wired electrical connections forced a shutdown and damaged some of the magnets, which had to be replaced. Engineers got it running again in October 2009 in what was described as "a cautious switch-on," and the first collisions occurred on March 30, 2010. Stay tuned. **Bonus question: An online bookmaker is offering 2 to 1 odds that the collider will reach full power in 2014. What are the odds that the collider's first discovery will be the existence of God?** The odds are 100 to 1. The odds are 11 to 10 that the first discovery will be dark matter and 8 to 1 that it will be black holes.

WHAT'S THE MOST AMBITIOUS ENGINEERING PROJECT EVER?

The Gotthard Base Tunnel. Some 2,000 people are digging the longest tunnel ever—thirty-five miles—through the base of rocky mountains in the Swiss Alps at a cost of $8 billion. They've been working since 1996 and hope to finish digging in 2011, but the tunnel isn't expected to be ready for traffic until 2017. When it is, it will cut twenty-five miles, or one hour, off the trip from Zurich to Milan. In the meantime, they're digging—on good days through as much as eighty-two feet of rock, on bad days, only about three feet.

IS IT POSSIBLE FOR A CAR TO TRAVEL 1,000 MPH?

By the time you read this, it may have happened. The British team that broke the sound barrier when it set the current land speed record of 763 mph in 1997 is building a $15 million Bloodhound Supersonic Car, which has three different engines: (1) a hybrid rocket engine for initial thrust, (2) a jet engine from a warplane for power, and (3) a typical gas-powered engine to start the car and move peroxide fuel into the rocket engine. The team hopes to break the 1,000-mph mark in 2011. The ultimate goal: 1,050 mph—even faster than a speeding (.357) bullet, which travels at 971 mph. **What you can do:** You can buy a real fast car. The fastest street-legal car in the world is the SSC Ultimate Aero, which has a maximum speed of 257 mph and goes from 0 to 60 in 2.7 seconds. At $654,400, it's the sixth-most-expensive car in the world. The most expensive, the Bugatti Veyron, costs $1.7 million and maxes out at 253 mph.

WHAT'S 1,000 MILES NORTHEAST OF HAWAII, DOUBLES IN SIZE EVERY TEN YEARS, AND IS ABOUT TWICE THE SIZE OF TEXAS?

A swirling accumulation of garbage, the largest of at least a few giant trash patches in the world's oceans. Like the others, this one, discovered in 1997, is made up largely of billions and billions of plastic pieces as well as refuse from fishing gear and other garbage. Scientists, who have found plastic in the tissues of fish that feed on plankton in the area, are studying this patch to determine its effects on the environment.

HOW MUCH WATER DO AMERICANS FLUSH DOWN THE TOILET EVERY SECOND, AND WHY IS THAT A WASTE—IN MORE WAYS THAN ONE?

They flush 64,000 gallons. Environmental activists would have us do what others do around the world: Use it to fertilize plants and crops. Urine is collected to be used as fertilizer by more than 600,000 Chinese in seventeen provinces, by communities in seventeen African countries, and by 130 Swedish households, which has sent more than 40,000 gallons a year for more than a decade to spray on crops. If you live in America and think this is a good idea, don't hold your breath. There is no organized effort to recycle urine on a large scale. **What you can do:** A severe toilet leak can waste as many as 500 gallons of water per day. Put a dye tablet in your toilet tank. If the colored water makes it from your toilet tank to your toilet bowl, you have a leak. Fixing it will probably cost you a $2 seal and about five minutes of your time.

HOW MANY GALLONS OF WATER ARE USED TO MAKE A DIAPER, A COTTON T-SHIRT, A REAM OF WHITE PAPER AND A PAIR OF LEATHER SHOES?

Respectively: 214, 719, 1,321, and 2,113. And it takes 2,886 gallons of water to make a pair of jeans. Why do cotton products require so much water? Cotton doesn't require a lot of water to grow, but it takes a lot of water to make it into a fabric. It takes the same amount of water to make thirteen pairs of jeans as it does to make a midsize car (39,090 gallons). **Bonus question: How much water is used every day for golf course irrigation in the United States?** Two billion gallons. Environmentalists urge managers of coastal golf courses to use Paspalum turf, which survives brief droughts and likes brackish water. **What you can do:** Figure out your water footprint by using the water footprint calculator at the website for the Netherlands-based Water Footprint Network. Then try to reduce it.

E. COLI HAS A PRETTY LOUSY REPUTATION. IS IT GOOD FOR ANYTHING?

Apparently so. A California company has genetically engineered it to create biodiesel. When the modified *E. coli* is mixed with sugarcane and water, the result, which floats to the top of the water and is skimmed off, is the same hydrocarbon configuration as petroleum. The company says this fuel could cost only $50 per barrel.

NEXT YOU'RE GOING TO SAY THAT YOU CAN MAKE BIODIESEL FROM CHICKEN FEATHERS!

Yep. Scientists at the University of Nevada–Reno have made biodiesel from chicken feathers, more specifically from the fat in chicken feather meal, which farmers use as a fertilizer or as animal feed. If America's feather meal was used for this purpose, 150 million gallons of biodiesel could be produced per year—still a drop in the oil barrel. Other scientists have made bioethanol from watermelons, 20 percent of which sit in the field because they aren't pretty enough to sell. If that weren't enough, the same researchers made biodiesel from coffee grounds after an engineering professor there noticed a sheen of oil floating atop a cup of stale coffee. The scientists gathered fifty pounds of coffee grounds from Starbucks stores and found that 10 to 15 percent of it was oil, which they extracted and made into biodiesel. (And, yes, the exhaust does smell like coffee.) They concluded it can be made for about $1 per gallon, but all of the coffee grounds in the world would make only a tiny dent to relieve the demand for oil.

WHERE IS THE WORLD'S MOST ENERGY-EFFICIENT SKYSCRAPER?

In Guangzhou, a city about seventy-five miles northwest of Hong Kong in southern China. The seventy-one-story Pearl River Tower, built by state-owned China National Tobacco Corporation and scheduled to be finished in 2011, is expected to cut carbon dioxide consumption by as much as 58 percent compared with other buildings of its size. The building will collect solar energy and use a chilled water system to heat and cool it, and will be dehumidified with energy from four wind turbines.

FOR MORE THAN A CENTURY, PSYCHOLOGISTS HAVE OFFERED THE WORLD A HOST OF PSYCHOLOGICAL EXPLANATIONS FOR OUR DREAMS: THEY ALLOW US TO ACT OUT OUR PRIMAL WANTS. THEY HIGHLIGHT OUR FEARS. THEY HELP US WORK THROUGH OUR PROBLEMS. WHAT IF ALL THAT IS A BUNCH OF HOOEY?

A new crop of scientists say dreaming may help us more with physiological issues than with psychological ones. Dreaming, one psychiatrist says, is a way we tune up our minds for consciousness. After all, they say, if our dreams are full of psychological meanings intended to help us better understand ourselves, why do we forget so many of them? The research has triggered a lot of debate.

Six

ANIMAL KINGDOM

W hat is it about animals that fascinate us so much? Well, let's count the ways: There's a lizard that may hold the key to something better than duct tape. There's a beetle that can carry 850 times its weight. There's a deer that refuses to acknowledge the end of the Cold War and a spider that can survive without food for three years. This chapter also looks at bloodsucking creatures, including one researchers once thought was selfless but now know is really pretty selfish. There's a new reason to fear—and admire—termites and ants. And who doesn't want to know the answer to this question: If you found a well-preserved woolly mammoth, what could you trade it for?

THE BERLIN WALL CAME DOWN IN 1989, BUT WHAT CREATURE STILL REFUSES TO CROSS THE BORDER?

Red deer called Ahornia, which live in Germany's Bavarian Forest National Park. For years a tall electric fence ran along the Czech-German border, keeping Ahornia on the German side. When the fence came down, animals such as lynx, fox, and elk almost immediately crossed the border and populated both sides, but not Ahornia. Biologists who track the deer with electric collars say Ahornia that approach the border stop and remain in Germany—even those born long after the wall came down. One theory: These deer use—and don't stray from—old trails that were made before the wall came down. **Bonus question: In 2009, when the rock band U2 did a free concert commemorating the twentieth anniversary of the fall of the Berlin Wall, why were so many people so upset?** Concert organizers built a six-and-a-half-foot-high wall to keep people without tickets from entering the venue.

BY FAR THE BEST-PRESERVED WOOLLY MAMMOTH EVER FOUND, IN MAY 2007 IN NORTHWESTERN SIBERIA, WAS PROMPTLY STOLEN AND SOLD TO AN UNSUSPECTING SHOP OWNER. WHAT DID THE THIEVES GET FOR IT?

Two snowmobiles and a year's supply of food. A reindeer herder initially found it, but sometime after that two men stole it and took it to a store where they traded it for the snowmobiles. The reindeer herder found it displayed at the store and alerted local police, who alerted scientists. The scientists took it to a museum, where they studied it before the 40,000-year-old creature endured a three-day autopsy on a Plexiglas light table in a genetics laboratory in St. Petersburg, Russia. It was so well preserved in ice and snow that the scientists found its last meal—of plants—in its mouth.

WHEN IS A MALE FISH ALSO A FEMALE FISH?

When it's in one of eight major river basins, including the Mississippi, the Columbia, and the Colorado, where scientists believe pollution from farms and sewage treatment plants is causing male fish to produce female eggs. The scientists refer to fish in this predicament as not male or female but "intersex," and during a nine-year study they discovered that 44 percent of the largemouth and smallmouth bass dissected were intersex. At some sites, nine out of ten largemouth bass turned out to be intersex, causing biologists to wonder whether the species can sustain itself. The researchers caution that they can't positively pinpoint what's causing this transformation, but they strongly suspect it's pollution. **What you can do:** There still are a lot of great places to catch largemouth bass, and here are some fishing tips: Largemouth bass like warm water, so fish in ten feet of water or less. Use a monofilament line and live bait in clear water, but in murky water use a bright lure—six- to eight-inch plastic worms work best.

DUCT TAPE, ONE OF THE MOST ESSENTIAL ITEMS IN ANY TOOLBOX, MAY HAVE ITS DOMINANCE THREATENED THANKS TO WHAT LIZARD?

The gecko. It turns out that geckos have millions of incredibly tiny and sticky hairs attached to their toes, allowing them to walk on walls and ceilings with little effort. That discovery led an engineering professor at Stanford to create a prototype for a reusable and extremely strong tape that leaves no sticky residue. How strong is this tape? One of the researchers who studies geckos used it to stick his fifty-pound daughter to a window. More than fifty patents are pending that may lead to a product or two before long.

WITH THE NATION'S CURRENT FASCINATION WITH VAMPIRES, WHICH MEMBERS OF THE ANIMAL KINGDOM, BESIDES THE OBVIOUS (FEMALE MOSQUITOES AND VAMPIRE BATS), SUCK BLOOD?

Here's an incomplete list:

1. The vampire finch, while in flight, pecks on the hind parts of seabirds.
2. Candiru catfish, which look like whiskery eels, draw blood from the gills of fish.
3. As many as 2,000 species of fleas feed on the blood of mammals and birds.

4. Aquatic and land-based leeches have been known to wiggle into any crevice and hole, including nostrils and urethras, to make a home and find blood.
5. A bird called the oxpecker has been known for years as a friend to buffalo, rhinos, giraffes and other animals because it sits on their backs and removes ticks from their hides. But researchers have found that oxpeckers also are pains in the you-know-what. They stick their beaks in the wounds created by those ticks and slurp up blood.

Vampire bats, by the way, don't *suck* blood. Their teeth and tongue form a tube that works like a catheter and very efficiently draws out blood, which, by the way, happens to be 95 percent water. The other 5 percent is mostly made up of proteins and sugars.

RESEARCHERS HAVE LONG KNOWN THAT PIGS ARE PRETTY SMART. THEY CAN HERD SHEEP, OPEN AND CLOSE CAGES, FOLLOW OTHER PIGS ON THE TRAIL OF FOOD, AND DECEIVE IF IT SUITS THEM. WHAT RECENT DISCOVERY HAS FURTHER ENHANCED THEIR CLEVER REPUTATION?

It seems that pigs can use mirrors to find food. Young pigs exposed to mirrors for as briefly as five hours figured out if they saw a food bowl in the mirror the food was behind them. After that exposure to the mirrors, it took pigs an average of twenty-three seconds to find the food while pigs that had never before seen a mirror were stumped. They continually bumped into it or went behind it in an attempt to find the food. Despite this impressive feat, the researchers cannot say whether the pigs recognized themselves in the mirror, a sign of advanced intelligence exhibited by apes and dolphins.

WHAT'S THE RELATIVE R-VALUE FOR THE BLUBBER THAT ALLOWS POLAR BEARS TO SURVIVE THE COLD SEASON?

The polar bear's blubber is equivalent to about ten wool sweaters. This superinsulating blubber allows polar bears to survive at minus 40 degrees F. At that temperature, motor oil has the consistency of hot tar and copper wire becomes brittle. **Bonus question: What shocking thing happened to three spectacled bears in a German zoo?** They went bald, and no one is quite sure why. But there was an upside to the follicular disaster, at least for the zoo. The bears, which are native to South America and are sometimes called Andean bears, attracted hordes of visitors. **What you can do:** It's probably not even possible to wear ten sweaters. For extreme cold weather, wear layers of clothing. Start with thermal under-wear. Next, put on wool pants and sweaters—which, unlike cotton, repel moisture and make a great second layer—under a parka or lined overcoat. Wool hats and scarves are warm but itchy, so try hats and scarves made of cashmere.

TINY, JAMES BOND–LIKE TRACKING DEVICES ARE PROVIDING BIOLOGISTS WITH INFORMATION THAT IS CHANGING THE WAY THEY VIEW INSECTS, BIRDS, FISH, AND OTHER CREATURES. WHAT ARE SOME OF THE MORE SURPRISING THINGS THEY'VE LEARNED?

A German biologist who bothered to glue transmitters weighing .3 grams to the bodies of fourteen dragonflies and then tracked them inside a single-engine Cessna found that dragonflies fly only during warm daylight hours, won't fly if it's too windy, and actually schedule rest days. (By the way, how much is .3 grams? Take a dollar bill and cut it into thirds. One of those pieces weighs .3 grams.) A biologist who implanted transmitters in black racer snakes in Maine discovered that female snakes will travel as many as three miles to lay their eggs, a long trek for something that gets around by crawling on its belly. Another biologist discovered a "salmon superhighway" near Newfoundland, where the fish socialize before heading to feeding grounds near Greenland.

FOR YEARS ENTOMOLOGISTS MARVELED AT HOW EFFICIENTLY ANTS CARRIED AWAY THEIR DEAD BRETHREN BEFORE PATHOGENS COULD INFECT THE COMMUNITY. RESEARCHERS THOUGHT THEY KNEW WHY, BUT THEY DIDN'T. WHAT HAVE THEY RECENTLY LEARNED?

Researchers theorized that ants were especially good at detecting decomposing bodies, but it turns out that they're especially good at detecting two specific chemicals that ants emit while they're alive. These chemicals disappear within one hour of death, and ant workers immediately realize the chemicals are gone, and they find their dead comrades and remove them. **Bonus question: What shocking thing did entomologists learn about army ants, vicious marauders that won't think twice about killing their own kind during battle?** They might be vicious killers, but army ants will adopt into their colonies ants whose queens have been killed during wars. The adopted ants lose their old-colony odor and become part of the new colony's family within days.

CHARLOTTE'S WEB ASIDE, ENTOMOLOGISTS KNOW SPIDERS TO BE FEROCIOUS PREDATORS. ARE THERE ANY KINDER AND GENTLER TYPES?

It turns out that a tropical spider, a.k.a. *Bagheera kiplingi*, is a vegetarian. A couple of entomologists doing field studies in Mexico were checking out a spider that landed on an acacia plant loaded with ants. They expected at least one of the ants to be dead meat. Instead, the spider avoided the ants and went for a leaf—the first scientific sighting of a spider feeding deliberately on plants. The scientists witnessed the same thing in Costa Rica.

WHAT'S THE STRONGEST ANIMAL IN THE WORLD?

The rhinoceros beetle is—in relation to its size, that is. The beetle, which grows to slightly more than two inches long and one ounce, can lift up to 850 times its weight, or slightly more than fifty-three pounds—the equivalent of a bushel of canning tomatoes or an average seven-year-old boy. To put that into perspective, if a 154-pound person had the strength of the rhinoceros beetle, he would likely be able to lift an object as heavy as 130,900 pounds, such as an M1 Abrams tank, a Trident II nuclear submarine missile, an empty Boeing 737—or 850 154-pound individuals.

THE ALASKAN UPIS BEETLE FREEZES AT ABOUT MINUS 19 DEGREES F BUT CAN SURVIVE AT MINUS 100 DEGREES F. HOW IS THAT POSSIBLE?

Inside the slender black beetle is a sugar-based antifreeze that is incredibly effective at resisting ice buildup. When it comes to surviving in the cold, ice—more than temperature—is the real threat because it can disrupt the liquid in an animal's cells, leading to the destruction of their tissues. Years ago biologists discovered that some animals—from fish to insects—survive thanks to different types of antifreeze in their bodies. While other beetles have a protein-based antifreeze, the Alaskan Upis beetle's sugar-based antifreeze is as good as it gets.

ALASKAN UPIS BEETLES ARE HARDCORE, NO DOUBT, BUT WHAT'S THE TOUGHEST, MOST RESILIENT CREATURE ON EARTH?

There may be some debate here, but many scientists give the nod to microscopic blobs commonly called water bears, which can live anywhere from the world's tallest mountains to ocean bottoms. Water bears, also known as tardigrades, owe their toughness to their ability to tolerate extreme dehydration. Swedish scientists dehydrated 3,000 or so of them, sent them into space and exposed them to all the harshness that it has to offer. After they returned, they were rehydrated. Most went on living as if they had spent a few hours in the luggage hold of a 747.

WHAT SINGLE-CELL CREATURE COMMUNICATES IN TWO LANGUAGES, LOVES COMPANY, IDENTIFIES FRIEND FROM FOE AND SPREADS MISINFORMATION?

A bacterium. Scientists now know that bacteria communicate with each other by sending out signals using molecules called autoinducers. Bacteria like to congregate in big groups, and when the groups reach a certain size, they attack whatever they're near. This attack is the beginning of infection. Scientists want to figure out how to jam the bacteria's communication signals so they can't assemble in large enough groups to launch an attack. Researchers hope this knowledge will lead to better drugs to fight bacteria that harm people and animals.

HOW LONG CAN TARANTULAS LIVE WITHOUT FOOD?

Three years. Tarantulas like food, and they eat a diverse diet that includes insects, mammals, and amphibians, but a handful of the nearly 900 species can survive on water alone for three years. Tarantulas, by the way, might scare you, but they can't kill you—unless you're small enough for them to eat. **What you can do:** Tarantulas make good pets because they're low maintenance, but they don't like other tarantulas very much, so don't put more than one in an aquarium. They don't need much space, so the aquarium can be as small as two and a half or five gallons. Layer the bottom with some soil and vermiculite. Add some bark for a hiding place and a shallow water dish so they won't drown. They like it warm—75 degrees or more—and dry. If it's not humid, the aquarium won't get moldy, and you'll have to clean it only once a year.

MOST PEOPLE KNOW BLUE WHALES ARE THE WORLD'S LARGEST MAMMALS, BUT WHAT'S THE SMALLEST MAMMAL?

Adult bumblebee bats, which live in Thailand and weigh about 2 grams—or .07 ounces. What weighs .07 ounces? Take a slice of bread and cut it into ten identical pieces. One of those pieces weighs about .07 ounces.

ARE THERE ANY PLACES IN THE WORLD WHERE SNAKES DON'T LIVE IN THE WILD?

Yes—Ireland, New Zealand, Iceland, Greenland, and Antarctica. These places might seem to have little in common, but there is one thing: They are all surrounded by water, and no snake has migrated long distances over water to a new home. What's more, snakes are pretty adaptable—they live in deserts, grasslands, forests, and mountains—but they can't survive in places where the ground is always frozen. Which explains why snakes wouldn't make it in Greenland and Antarctica even if they did have the stamina to swim there. **What you can do:** Snakes have a reputation as biters, even though most want nothing to do with people. But if a snake bites you, wash the wound with lots of soap and water and seek medical treatment. Don't do the following things you were taught in boy scouts: Cut and suck out the poison, or use ice, alcohol, or tourniquets. They can do more harm than good.

RATS HAVE A REPUTATION AS PLAGUE STARTERS, AMONG OTHER THINGS, SO WHY ARE THEY GIVEN HERO STATUS IN THE AFRICAN NATIONS OF TANZANIA AND MOZAMBIQUE?

About fifty rats, dubbed HeroRATs, have been trained to sniff out land mines in those countries, and they're very good at it. A Belgian man, the brains behind the rats, says the breed he chose, the African giant pouched rat, is easy to train, cheap to breed, and too light to detonate a mine if it steps on one.

AFTER THE FIDDLER CRAB LEAVES ITS HOME TO FORAGE FOR FOOD, HOW DOES IT FIND ITS WAY BACK?

By counting. The crab keeps track of its stride to measure the distance between its home and its destination—the first time scientists have proven that an animal uses this method to keep from getting lost. Scientists figured this out by tricking the crabs, putting a slippery sheet of acetate in its path. With some strides, the crabs made no progress, but they didn't realize it, so when they expected to reach their burrows, they stopped, not realizing they stopped short.

THE STAR-NOSED MOLE—ARGUABLY THE MOST BIZARRE-LOOKING CREATURE ON EARTH, WITH INCREDIBLY LONG, WHITE, FINGERNAIL-LIKE CLAWS, A HAIRY BODY, AND A PINK SNOUT THAT

RESEMBLES TWO SEA STARS STUCK TOGETHER—IS ALSO VIRTUALLY BLIND, BUT WHY DOESN'T IT NEED A HANDOUT?

It holds the distinction of being the fastest hunter and scavenger among all mammals. Its nose's tentacles—five times more sensitive than human fingertips—search as many as thirteen spots per second for insects and other prey. In 230 milliseconds—faster than a blink of an eye—the mole figures out if it wants to eat what it found and then either consumes it or moves on.

TERMITES, THOUGH FEARED, MOSTLY LIVE IN OBSCURITY, MUNCHING AWAY AT YOUR TREE STUMP OR YOUR GARAGE OR YOUR HOUSE. BUT WHEN THEY'RE NOT WORKING, WHAT DO THEY DO IN THEIR SPARE TIME?

They hang out at their houses, which are not made of anything they like to eat. Termites live in dirt mounds, which can be twenty feet tall—as tall as a two-story house. And termites believe in home security: Some protect their mounds by spraying intruders with chemicals from nozzles on their heads while others have powerful mandibles that can behead ants and other unwelcome insects.

ARGENTINE ANTS HAVE BEEN CALLED ONE OF THE WORLD'S MOST DESTRUCTIVE PESTS, WIPING OUT CROPS AND OTHER ANT SPECIES AND INVADING HOMES. THE TINY ANTS HAVE TRAVELED FROM THEIR NATIVE ARGENTINA TO EVERY CONTINENT EXCEPT ANTARCTICA. HOW HAVE THEY BECOME SO DOMINANT?

They are the ultimate team players. Argentine ants cooperate with each other—sharing food with ants that are unfamiliar to them, for example—more than just about any other insect. Researchers say the ants' genes make them virtually identical and un-competitive—with each other, that is. **What you can do:** If Argentine ants get into your house, use an insecticide that includes Cypermethrin. To keep them from getting in, keep the ground around your house dry—they love moist soil—and weed around the foundation to reduce hiding places.

ARGUABLY THE NASTIEST OF INSECTS, WASPS HAVE EARNED THEIR REPUTATION, BUT DO THEY HAVE A HEART?

Somewhat. One wasp, *Dinocampus coccinellae*, kidnaps ladybugs and forces them to incubate its eggs. According to the entomologist who's studied this, the wasps lay their eggs *on* the abducted ladybugs, which keep the wasp larvae warm between their legs. After the larvae hatch and move on, the wasps, as a reward, release the ladybugs from captivity—something they wouldn't do if they just happened upon a ladybug. **Bonus question: Does something like this happen elsewhere in the animal kingdom?** Yes—and with dire consequences. Magpies are forced to babysit the chicks of great spotted cuckoos, which check up on the magpies and kill the ones that aren't doing their jobs well enough.

SCIENTISTS RECENTLY LEARNED BEES HAVE SOMETHING IN COMMON WITH PEOPLE. WHAT?

Bees can remember human faces, though the scientists assume the bees just think they're seeing strange-looking flowers, not faces. The researchers made the discovery during an experiment in which they set up a display of pictures of faces behind bowls of sugar water and pictures of nonfaces behind bowls of plain water. After several hours, 75 percent of the time the bees figured out that the bowls in front of the pictures of faces contained the sugar water, which they like. The scientists concluded that the bees pieced together the ears, nose, mouth, and eyes in the pictures and identified a pattern they were able to recognize time after time. **What you can do:** If you have trouble recognizing faces, you may suffer from a little-known disorder called prosopagnosia, or face blindness. The disorder keeps people from recognizing the faces of even family members or close friends or from mistaking a stranger from a friend. Some face-blind people don't watch TV or movies because they can't keep track of the characters. Think you suffer from face blindness? Complete a questionnaire at www.faceblind.org.

WHAT CREATURE CAN GROW TO FIFTY FEET LONG AND TWENTY-TWO TONS AND HAS 90,000 BRETHREN BUT IS RARELY SEEN?

The Bryde's whale. The whale, named after a Norwegian whaler who pronounced his name BROO-duhz, is perhaps best known for its huge appetite, consuming about 1,300 pounds of fish per day. Spread out over the Atlantic, Pacific, and Indian oceans, the whales can dive to a depth of 1,000 feet and are elusive, making them hard to study. And because they are relatively slender and aren't endowed with much blubber, whalers haven't pursued them, so they are poorly understood by scientists as well as fishermen.

NORTHERN ELEPHANT SEALS ARE RENOWNED FOR THEIR PACIFIC OCEAN SWIMS, WHICH CAN LAST AS LONG AS EIGHT MONTHS, WITH 90 PERCENT OF THAT TIME SPENT ON DEEP-SEA DIVES. WHEN DO THEY SLEEP?

It turns out they catch a few winks during those dives, particularly during "drift dives," in which the seals slow down and descend like a falling leaf. Researchers who tracked six young seals found that after they dove to a depth of 500 feet, they rolled onto their backs and coasted for about ten minutes. Their dives sometimes ended with a collision on the ocean bottom, a sign that they were sleeping.

GUIDE DOGS FOR THE BLIND ARE BY FAR THE MOST COMMON "SERVICE ANIMALS" RECOGNIZED BY THE AMERICANS WITH DISABILITIES ACT. WHAT ARE SOME OF THE RAREST ONES?

A man in Missouri who suffers from psychosis uses a parrot to help calm him down. A bonnet macaque monkey recognizes a Missouri woman's panic attacks before she does and must be present whenever she gets behind the wheel of her car. In fact, it sits on her lap with one hand on the steering wheel when she drives. And you can add cats, miniature horses, ferrets, iguanas, and ducks to the approved list of service animals. **What you can't do:** If you own a business, including a restaurant, you cannot exclude a service animal unless you have reason to believe it poses a threat to others.

WHEN DID WILD CATS BECOME HOUSE CATS?

A lot earlier than previously thought. Archaeologists knew of statues and paintings of cats in Israel and Egypt that date to about 1600 BC, a sign that people back then lived with cats. But a cat found buried with a person on the Mediterranean island of Cyprus in about 7500 BC has caused scientists to believe cats and people have had special relationships for at least 9,500 years and maybe longer.

CAPTIVE TIGERS HAVE KILLED AT LEAST FIFTY-TWO PEOPLE AND INJURED HUNDREDS IN THE PAST DECADE. HAS THAT CURBED THEIR APPEAL AS PETS?

Not at all. The number of captive tigers in the United States alone (about 4,900) exceeds the number in the wild in Asia (about 4,000). At least 13,000 live in captivity worldwide. **What you can do:** Want to own a tiger? Take these steps: (1) know your local and state laws; (2) get training on how to act around it; (3) find a veterinarian who will treat it; (4) build secure housing for it; (5) learn how to bottle-feed a cub so you can bond with it; (6) buy from a reputable breeder; and (7) give it a lot of thought. Tigers can grow to 500 pounds and most zoos and sanctuaries have too many and won't accept yours should you need to give it up.

THERE ARE ONLY TWO EGG-LAYING MAMMALS LEFT IN THE WORLD. WHAT ARE THEY, AND WHAT DOES NEW RESEARCH SAY ABOUT HOW THEY SURVIVED WHEN OTHERS DID NOT?

The survivors are the duckbill platypus, which looks like a beaver with a dark brown duckbill, and an anteater called an echidna. Researchers say these egg-laying mammals and other similar creatures dominated Australia until marsupials invaded and wiped them out. The duckbill platypus and the echidna survived because they adapted to life in the water—a place where marsupials did not want to follow.

WHAT DO SCIENTISTS KNOW ABOUT TOUCANS' BEAKS BESIDES THE FACT THAT THEY'RE REALLY, REALLY LONG?

They help keep the toucans cool. Recent research, using a thermal imaging camera, shows that toucans use their bills like automobile radiators, with blood as the coolant.

LLAMAS ARE HIGH-MAINTENANCE CREATURES THAT WON'T THINK TWICE ABOUT SPITTING ON SOMEONE WHO ANNOYS THEM, BUT HOW MIGHT THEY SOMEDAY MAKE AN ENORMOUS IMPACT ON MANKIND?

Llamas and their cousins—camels and alpacas—create antibodies that strengthen immune systems, and scientists are studying these animals with the hope that they will find new treatments for human diseases. Mammals have different types of antibodies, which come in different sizes and compositions and do different things. And scientists hope these antibodies, which are much smaller than antibodies in people, can fit into snug places where other antibodies cannot.

HUMANS HAVE DISCOVERED 1.8 MILLION OR SO LIVING SPECIES SINCE WE STARTED KEEPING TRACK IN 1758. IS THIS JOB ABOUT WRAPPING UP BY NOW?

Uh, no. In 2007 alone, scientists discovered 18,516 species: 9,411 insects; 2,830 mammals, birds, amphibians, reptiles, and fish; 1,194 spiders, ticks, and scorpions; 1,807 snails, clams, squid, crabs, lobsters, barnacles, and shrimp; 631 bacteria; and 591 protozoa. And in case you're wondering, that doesn't even include fungi. Most biologists believe we've identified only a small fraction of the world's living things. **Bonus question: How many of the 1.8 million species we know about are insects?** More than 1 million.

CHARLES DARWIN OBSERVED IT WHEN HE VISITED THE GALÁPAGOS ISLANDS: ANIMALS THERE ARE LESS AGGRESSIVE AND LESS AFRAID. WHAT'S THE EXPLANATION FROM MODERN SCIENTISTS? Islands in general are places where animals usually have less to fear because there are fewer species—and fewer predators. That means most residents aren't wasting energy—and stressing out while—running, fighting, and hiding. Not only that, but over the generations, skittish animals will bear fewer offspring while tame, fearless animals will bear more and outnumber them.

Seven

UNDERDOGS, STOCKY MARATHONERS AND DIVING GOALIES

S ports fans, this one's for you, but it's not the place where you'll find batting averages, shooting percentages, and quarterback ratings. This chapter answers the kinds of questions you would never think to ask, such as: If you're a soccer goalie, which way do you dive if you want to stop the most shots? Why are major league baseballs so pampered, especially in Denver? Why are times for marathon races increasing? How can the world's most rabid soccer nation live in a country with mediocre soccer players?

IS IT TRUE THAT UNDERDOGS HAVE MORE MOTIVATION BECAUSE THEY HAVE A CHIP ON THEIR SHOULDERS AND WANT TO KNOCK OFF THE FAVORED TEAMS?

Not really. The favorites, it turns out, try 30 percent harder when they face underdogs a new study shows. Favorites try harder because they have more to lose, and they fear the humiliation of losing to teams they should beat. The results of the study contradict the common belief that underdogs have more motivation than their competition, and the researchers say this applies far beyond sports. In fact, they arrived at their conclusion by administering a series of tests to college students. In one test, students were asked to do an incredibly mundane task: cross out vowels on documents. The students were competing against students from other colleges, and they always knew the identity of their competition. That information caused students from more academically prestigious colleges to try harder than groups of students that didn't know against whom they were competing. **What you can do:** If you're the underdog in whatever you do, there might be less pressure on you to win, but realize that the favorite probably is taking you seriously. Focus and try your best. Even if you don't win, you'll have no regrets.

SPEAKING OF UNDERDOGS, "MIRACLE ON ICE," THE STUNNING 4–3 VICTORY BY THE YOUNG, AMATEUR U.S. HOCKEY TEAM OVER THE VETERAN, PROFESSIONAL SOVIET TEAM IN THE 1980 WINTER OLYMPICS, IS REGARDED AS ONE OF THE GREATEST UPSETS IN SPORTS HISTORY AND HAS BEEN THE SUBJECT OF NUMEROUS BOOKS, BUT WHAT DON'T MOST PEOPLE KNOW ABOUT THE EVENT? The star of the 1980 Winter Olympics, Eric Heiden, who won five speed skating gold medals, couldn't get a ticket to the game, but he was allowed to sit behind ABC broadcasters Al Michaels and Ken Dryden. ABC put Heiden's chair on a little platform, but he still couldn't see the game very well. Michaels, who became famous for saying "Do you believe in miracles? Yes!" at the end of the game, was picked to work that game because he was the only ABC sports announcer at the time who had ever called a hockey game and no one else wanted to do it. How many games had Michaels called before he did the U.S.-Soviet game? One—eight years earlier, at the 1972 Olympics in Sapporo, Japan.

WINTER OLYMPIANS OBVIOUSLY TRAIN FOR YEARS TO GET A CHANCE TO COMPETE FOR PRECIOUS MEDALS, BUT HOW MUCH TIME DO MEDAL WINNERS ACTUALLY SPEND PERFORMING THEIR EVENTS?

As few as twenty-six seconds for ski jumpers, including qualifying stages, and as many as twelve hours and forty-five minutes for curlers. Some of the other events where athletes compete for a very brief time: aerial skiing (thirty seconds on average), moguls skiing (forty-six seconds), 500-meter speed skating (one minute and ten seconds), super giant slalom alpine skiing (one minute and thirty-one seconds), and doubles luge (one minute and thirty-four seconds). Other Winter Olympic sports with the longest face time for athletes: hockey (eight hours) and fifty-kilometer cross-country skiing (two hours, six minutes, and twelve seconds). **Bonus questions #1: How many cross-country ski waxing technicians did Norway bring to the Vancouver Winter Olympics in 2010?** They brought twenty-two. **Bonus question #2: How many pairs of cross-country skis did Germany bring to Vancouver in 2010 for its twelve biathlon skiers?** They brought 450.

HOW PREPOSTEROUS IS IT TO SAY THAT THE BEST NATIONAL FOOTBALL LEAGUE QUARTERBACKS ARE ALSO THE BEST-LOOKING QUARTERBACKS?

Not at all. One study showed photos of quarterbacks who played during the 1997 and 2007 seasons to sixty female Dutch college students. The students were then asked to rate the players' faces for attractiveness. The quarterbacks chosen as the most handsome by the college students also happened to have the best quarterback passing ratings. The researchers theorize that quarterbacks who are attractive are more likely to possess other positive traits, such as athleticism and intelligence. The latter two traits, by the way, help quarterbacks succeed.

WHO WAS THE MOST LOYAL SPORTS FAN?

If there is an answer in this book that's debatable, it might be this one, but here's a vote for Giles Pellerin. Pellerin attended every University of Southern California football game—797 in all—from September 25, 1926, to November 21, 1998, when, at ninety-one, he suffered a cardiac arrest at the USC-UCLA game and died in the parking lot of the Rose Bowl. USC, which piled up an amazing record of 535 wins, 225 losses, and 40 ties during Pellerin's attendance streak, lost 34–17 the day he died. A widower with no children, Pellerin, who traveled more than 650,000 miles over the years to watch the Trojans play, left $2 million and his Pasadena townhouse to USC. **An opposing point of view:** While Pellerin's feat is amazing, some say those who loyally follow bad teams are the real fans, and they point to Robert Lipson, who has attended every Kansas State University football home game since 1972 and every road conference game since 1973. Although Kansas State fielded good teams from 1993 to 2003, the other years' teams ranged from mediocre to bad. Lipson, who grew up in New York and enrolled at Kansas State in 1970, said he continues to go to the games even during the bad years because the team needs "the fans to help them." **What you can do:** Fan is short for fanatic, but security guards at sporting events have one rule for fans: Have fun, but don't do or say anything that might spoil the event for someone else.

IF YOU'RE A SOCCER GOALTENDER TRYING TO STOP A PENALTY KICK, WHICH WAY SHOULD YOU DIVE—LEFT OR RIGHT?

Neither. Stand in the middle of the goal and don't move. According to a recent paper by Israeli scientists who analyzed 286 penalty kicks, goalies dove to the right or to the left 94 percent of the time, even though staying in the center was the best option most of the time. Why the desire to move? Not moving would make them appear indecisive or even frozen with fear, the researchers theorized, and most didn't want to risk anyone thinking that.

WHICH COUNTRY LOVES SOCCER THE MOST—THE SOCCER POWERS OF ENGLAND, ITALY, GERMANY OR BRAZIL?

How about Norway? A journalist and an economist got together to crunch some numbers and found that the residents of Cyprus, Iceland, Scotland, and Norway—in that order—buy the most tickets for soccer matches per capita. Croatia, Norway, the Netherlands, and Uruguay watch the most soccer on television. Norwegians, who show up on both lists, have plenty of money and leisure time, compared with soccer fans in most other places. Its women's national team happens to be highly rated, but its men's team stinks.

IN 2010, MINNESOTA TWINS ALL-START CATCHER JOE MAUER SIGNED AN EIGHT-YEAR, $184-MILLION CONTRACT. WHAT PERK DOES HE RECEIVE THANKS TO MAJOR LEAGUE BASEBALL'S COLLECTIVE BARGAINING AGREEMENT?

Mauer, whose contract pays him the equivalent of $63,000 a day, can afford to feed a small city, but thanks to the collective bargaining agreement, he also receives $89.50 a day for meal money when the Twins are on the road. **Bonus question: Do you want to grow up to be a baseball player or a hedge fund manager?** The twenty-five highest-paid major league baseball players each made an average of $19 million in 2010 while the twenty-five highest-paid hedge fund managers each made an average of $1 billion in 2009—fifty-three times the average of the baseball players.

WHICH MAJOR LEAGUE BASEBALL TEAM KEEPS ITS BASEBALLS IN A HUMIDOR—AND WHY?

It's the Colorado Rockies, who play in Denver, the highest-altitude city in Major League Baseball. Playing in a high-altitude city is a big disadvantage for Rockies' pitchers because airborne baseballs meet less resistance there than do airborne baseballs elsewhere. Storing baseballs in humidors keeps them from drying out and losing weight, and wetter and heavier balls don't travel as far. A California physicist said keeping the balls at 50 percent humidity makes them less bouncy when they're hit so they won't travel as far. And the humidor seems to be working: Pitchers in the Rockies' ballpark gave up on average 6.50 runs every game before the use of the humidor and 5.46 afterward.

DENVER ISN'T THE ONLY PLACE WHERE BASEBALLS ARE PAMPERED, RIGHT?

Hours before every Major League Baseball game, ball boys rub mud—a very specific mud that originates from two secret places in a swamp in New Jersey—on baseballs, then towel them off. The swamp mud, plus a "magic" ingredient added by the company that provides the mud, gives the balls extra grip. The desire for less slippery baseballs first came in 1920, when a wild pitch killed a player. The brown gunk, also called rubbing mud, has been used in the big leagues since 1938 and actually made it into the Hall of Fame in 1968. **Bonus question: How many baseballs are used during an average big league game?** A big league ball usually lasts only three or four pitches before it's hit out of play—into the stands, over the home run fence, or into foul territory, where ball boys, players, or umpires often toss them to fans for souvenirs—and can't be retrieved. In an average game, nearly 100 balls are used. That comes to about 233,000 balls a season, give or take. **What you can do:** Want to catch a foul ball? You'll increase your chances if you: (1) buy a seat near the right or left field foul line, (2) bring a baseball glove, and (3) go after the rebound. Nine out of ten people who touch the ball first don't catch it.

THE AVERAGE MARATHON RACE TIMES HAVE INCREASED FROM ABOUT THREE AND A HALF HOURS FOR MEN AND FOUR HOURS FOR WOMEN IN 1980 TO ABOUT FOUR AND A QUARTER HOURS FOR MEN AND FOUR AND THREE-QUARTER HOURS FOR WOMEN TODAY. IS THIS BECAUSE WE'RE BECOMING FATTER AND SLOWER?

The population is becoming fatter, but that's not why marathon times keep increasing.

Attribute it to more weekend runners signing up for marathons. This is happening, among other reasons, because of the increasingly popular run-walk method, in which runners take walking breaks whenever they want. This makes marathons possible for people who otherwise would never have the stamina, strength, and endurance to finish a race. The New York City Marathon registers about 45,000 runners, and about 9,000 finish the race in five hours or more—three hours or more after the winners. **What you can do:** If you're a casual runner, there's no shame in walking during a marathon, but other runners have this message for you: Move to the side of the road and get out of the way.

WHEN MAJOR LEAGUE BASEBALL TEAMS SPEND TONS OF MONEY TO ATTRACT STAR PLAYERS, HOW MANY MORE GAMES DO THEY WIN ON AVERAGE THE FIRST SEASON THESE PLAYERS SUIT UP FOR THEM?

The question should read: How many more games do they *lose* on average? As a whole, teams that add to their payrolls tend to lose slightly more, and teams that dump big salaries tend to improve slightly. The twenty-eight teams that increased their payrolls by $20 million or more since 1990 won on average less than one additional game during their 162-game regular schedule. The forty-five teams that spent between $15 million and $19.99 million more lost slightly more games compared to the previous season. The eighteen teams that dumped at least $20 million in salary won about two additional games. The most extreme examples: The Texas Rangers got rid of $48.4 million in salaries from 2003 to 2004 and won an additional eighteen games, while the Detroit Tigers spent an additional $42.5 million in salaries from 2007 to 2008 and lost fourteen more games.

IN WHICH NORTH AMERICAN PROFESSIONAL SPORTS LEAGUE DOES MONEY SPENT ON PLAYERS AND WINS CORRELATE MORE OFTEN THAN NOT?

The National Hockey League. If 1 equals a direct correlation between payroll and winning and 0 represents absolutely no correlation, the NHL scores a .49—higher than in any other league—from 2000 to 2008. Teams that spend the most—the Detroit Red Wings, Pittsburgh Penguins, and New York Rangers—tend to make the playoffs the most. With a correlation score of .15, the National Football League comes in last.

AT WHAT AGE DO NATIONAL BASKETBALL ASSOCIATION PLAYERS PEAK?

At the ripe old ages of twenty-four and twenty-five. Players who are twenty-four or twenty-five help their teams achieve an average of 5.98 wins per season, according to a recent study that examined the impact of everyone who played in the league between 1977 and 2008. Players who are twenty years old account for 4.84 wins; twenty-one-year-olds, 5.32 wins; twenty-two-year-olds, 5.68 wins; twenty-three- and twenty-six-year-olds, 5.86 wins; twenty-seven-year-olds, 5.62 wins; twenty-eight-year-olds, 5.26 wins; and twenty-nine-year-olds, 4.78 wins.

WHAT PERCENTAGE OF MEN SAY THEY WOULDN'T DATE A WOMAN WHO DOESN'T FOLLOW FOOTBALL WELL ENOUGH TO KNOW WHO'S PLAYING IN THE SUPER BOWL?

Turns out that's a deal breaker for 20 percent of men. **Bonus question #1: What percentage of people watch the Super Bowl alone?** Nine percent. And 46 percent go to a Super Bowl party and watch with five or more people. **Bonus question #2: How many more tortilla chips are eaten during the two weeks surrounding the Super Bowl compared to any other two-week period?** Nineteen percent more.

THE NATIONAL FOOTBALL LEAGUE PRO BOWL IS THE ONLY MAJOR LEAGUE ALL-STAR GAME PLAYED AT THE END OF THE SEASON, AND PLAYERS WHO ARE NURSING INJURIES—EITHER REAL OR IMAGINED—OFTEN SKIP THE GAME WHILE THOSE WHO PARTICIPATE OFTEN DON'T PLAY HARD SO AS NOT TO RISK INJURY. HOW MUCH MONEY DO THE ATHLETES MAKE TO PLAY IN THE GAME?

It varies. And, it turns out it varies widely. In 2010, the players on the winning American Football Conference team earned at least $45,000 and the players on the losing National Football Conference team made at least $22,500. However, some players' contracts include lucrative incentives to be named to play in the Pro Bowl, such as the $1.5 million paid to defensive end Julius Peppers and the $200,000 paid to defensive end Jared Allen.

Eight

POLITICS, RELIGION AND OTHER THINGS YOU SHOULDN'T DISCUSS

Which topics of conversation are most likely to cause someone to throw a drink in your face at a dinner party? Which can keep you from getting that promotion? Which should you never discuss on a first date? As the title suggests, this chapter focuses on politics, religion, and other potentially taboo subjects, such as divorce and sex. (As you may have noticed, money, another topic your mother told you never to ask about, got its own chapter.) This one discloses secrets that Secret Service agents have spilled about presidents, the most—and least—politically corrupt states, the most outrageous political pardon in history, and the percentage of Americans who said they would act immorally to keep their jobs.

WHICH HAS BEEN THE MOST POLITICALLY CORRUPT STATE IN RECENT YEARS?

It depends how you measure it. From 1998 to 2007 Florida has had the most convicted public officials (824), followed by New York (704), Texas (565), Pennsylvania (555), California and Ohio (547), and Illinois (502), with a big drop-off to New Jersey (418), the District of Columbia (380), and Louisiana (332). But a per capita look at the numbers pushes DC to the top, with 66.9 convictions per 1 million residents, followed by the U.S. Virgin Islands (46.9), Guam (40.5), and then North Dakota (8.3), Alaska (7.9), Louisiana (7.5), Mississippi (7.4), and Montana (6.4). Why DC? Lots of politicians crammed into a geographically small area with relatively low population. If you take out DC and the territories, North Dakota comes out on top thanks to two large embezzlement cases by local officials.

THE LEAST CORRUPT STATE?

Nebraska, with only 12 convictions from 1998 to 2007 and a per capita rate of .7 convictions per 1 million people.

THE VAST MAJORITY OF SECRET SERVICE AGENTS, ESPECIALLY THE ONES WHO GUARD PRESIDENTS, ARE A TIGHT-LIPPED BUNCH. HAVE ANY SPILLED THE BEANS WITH ANYTHING JUICY?

Thankfully, yes. After their work is done, a few Secret Service agents, in books and interviews, have revealed the following tidbits about recent presidents:

- After his wife caught him in an uncompromising position with a secretary in the Oval Office, Lyndon B. Johnson had a warning buzzer installed to cover up his extramarital affairs.
- Richard Nixon, while on vacation in St. Martin, liked to go into the water, where he would stare at women, his eyes just above the surface of the water.
- Gerald Ford was a cheapskate who tipped like Ebenezer Scrooge and bummed coins from the agents who guarded him so he could buy newspapers.

- Jimmy Carter liked to be seen as a common man who carried his own luggage—so he often carried an empty suitcase, just for the photo op.
- Ronald Reagan packed a gun in his briefcase on his first trip to the Soviet Union in 1988.
- George H. W. Bush was incapable of sitting still for very long.
- Bill Clinton infuriated agents by entering crowds, where he was incredibly difficult to protect.
- George W. Bush liked to work out with Secret Service agents and other young, fit men, including cyclist Lance Armstrong. Because everyone knew Bush to be a sore loser, they always let him get the best of them.
- Barack Obama . . . details to come.

SPEAKING OF PRESIDENT OBAMA, HIS WORST NIGHTMARE CAME TRUE IN 2010, WHEN REPUBLICAN SCOTT BROWN BECAME A U.S. SENATOR, DEPRIVING SENATE DEMOCRATS—AND OBAMA—OF THE SIXTIETH VOTE THEY NEEDED TO PASS LEGISLATION WITHOUT REPUBLICAN SUPPORT. BROWN'S VICTORY IMMEDIATELY LED TO THE OVERHAUL OF OBAMA'S AMBITIOUS INITIATIVE TO PASS A NATIONAL HEALTH CARE BILL. WHAT DO OBAMA AND BROWN HAVE IN COMMON?

They're related—tenth cousins, to be exact. It turns out that both Obama's mother and Brown's mother descend from Richard Singletary of Haverhill, Massachusetts, according to the New England Historic Genealogical Society. Singletary died in 1687 at the unheard-of age back then of 102. His occupation? A politician, of course.

THE HEALTH CARE BILL OF 2009-10 HAS BEEN CALLED ONE OF THE MOST VOLUMINOUS PIECES OF LEGISLATION IN AMERICAN HISTORY—AS WELL AS SOME OTHER MUCH LESS COMPLIMENTARY THINGS. HOW BIG IS IT?

At 1,990 pages, the bill submitted by the House of Representatives was 765 pages longer than *War and Peace* and 648 pages longer than the health care bill introduced by President Bill Clinton in 1994. The single-sided copy version of the 2009 bill stood eight and a quarter inches high and weighed nearly twenty pounds, forcing some lawmakers to lug it around in a hand truck. Downloading it often caused computers to crash. Not to be outdone, the Senate version of the bill came in at 2,074 pages. But the lawmakers didn't stop there. The bill that passed was 2,562 pages.

OF OUR LAST TWELVE PRESIDENTS, WHOSE APPROVAL RATING ROSE AND PLUMMETED THE MOST IN HIS FIRST YEAR IN OFFICE?

George H. W. Bush's approval rating rose 29 points—from 51 percent to 80 percent—and Harry Truman's sank by 36 points, from 87 percent to 51 percent. Bush was helped by the fall of the Berlin Wall and the successful invasion by 25,000 U.S. troops to capture the Panamanian dictator Manuel Noriega. Truman, who proposed an unsuccessful and unpopular public health insurance plan during his first year in office, also had to deal with a labor crisis in which about 400,000 miners went on strike. Modern-day presidents whose approval ratings increased during their first year: Dwight Eisenhower, John F. Kennedy, Richard Nixon, and George W. Bush. Presidents whose approval ratings dipped: Lyndon Johnson, Gerald Ford, Jimmy Carter, Ronald Reagan, Bill Clinton, and Barack Obama. **Bonus question: The country may not have been ready for a national health care bill during Truman's presidency, but how did he get the last laugh?** He was the first enrollee in Medicare when Johnson signed it into law in 1965.

AMERICAN PRESIDENTS HAVE GOTTEN BAD PRESS FOR PARDONING EXILED SCOUNDRELS AND OTHER WELL-CONNECTED CROOKS, BUT WHAT'S UP WITH SOUTH KOREA'S PRESIDENT LEE MYUNG-BAK?

In 2008, he pardoned 341,864 politicians, businessmen, civil servants, and others, including 10,416 who committed criminal offenses. The most famous of the lucky 341,864 was Hyundai Motor Chairman Chung Mong-koo, who was convicted in 2007 of embezzling $90 million, some of which was used to bribe government officials. Lee said Chung and seventy-three other pardoned business leaders will help him revitalize South Korea's economy. The pardons became effective on August 15, known in South Korea as Liberation Day, which marks the end of Japanese colonial rule.

WHICH COUNTRY HAS THE BEST VOTER TURNOUT AND WHICH HAS THE WORST?

A look at 154 recent presidential or parliamentary elections shows Turkmenistan, a former Soviet republic, had the highest turnout with 99 percent, followed by the African nation of Rwanda (98 percent), Russia (97 percent), and Australia (95 percent). The first three of those nations put extreme pressure on their citizens to vote while Australians face a $20 fine if they don't vote. Egyptians face no fine, and in 2005, only 23 percent bothered to vote in an election widely viewed as corrupt. **What you can do:** The best time of the day to vote is midmorning and midafternoon. Not when folks are stopping at the polls in large numbers on their way to work, during their lunch breaks or on the way home from work.

WHAT'S THE MOST ANYONE HAS PAID (PER VOTE) TO WIN AN ELECTION?

In the priciest self-financed campaign in U.S. history, Michael Bloomberg spent $102 million—or $174 per vote—to win a third term as New York City mayor in 2009. Bloomberg, whose fortune has been estimated at $17.5 billion, spent $74 million ($99 per vote) to win the mayor's job in 2001 and $85.1 million ($112 per vote) in 2005. In 2009, though he faced a low-key candidate who waged a poorly organized campaign Bloomberg won by only five percentage points because of his unpopular opposition of term limits in the city. To compare Bloomberg's spending with other politicians, President Barack Obama spent a staggering $760,369,688 to win in 2008, but that came to only $11.37 per vote. Ten U.S. senators spent more per vote in 2008 than Obama, with Senator Mark Begich of Alaska spending the most per vote, $29.48. Senator Carl Levin of Michigan in 2008 spent the least per vote—$1.91. **What you can do:** If you want to find out how much money federal lawmakers receive to run their campaigns and where that money comes from, go to the Federal Election Commission's website. State and local electoral offices have similar information for state and local lawmakers.

PRESIDENT BARACK OBAMA, WHO VOWED TO TAKE THE POLITICS OUT OF GOVERNMENT, ATTENDED HOW MANY FUND-RAISERS FOR THE DEMOCRATIC PARTY AND ITS CANDIDATES DURING HIS FIRST YEAR AS PRESIDENT?
Twenty-six—twenty more than his predecessor, George W. Bush, attended during his first year as president.

PRESIDENT RICHARD NIXON WAS FOND OF MAKING DECLARATIONS, SUCH AS WHEN HE SAID THE UNITED STATES SHOULD CURE CANCER BY 1976. WHAT OTHER DECLARATION WAS WAY OFF THE MARK?
In January 1974 Nixon said, "At the end of this decade, in 1980, the United States will not be dependent on any other country for the energy we need to provide our jobs, to heat our homes and to keep our transportation moving." In 2009, Americans used 19.5 million barrels per day of petroleum products. Of those, 11.1 million, or 57 percent, were imported.

NOT TO PILE ON NIXON, BUT WHEN IT COMES TO PRESIDENTS TAKING RESPONSIBILITY FOR BLUN-DERS, HE ISN'T EXACTLY A PARAGON. HOW LONG DID IT TAKE HIM TO APOLOGIZE FOR WATERGATE?
He never actually did apologize—at least not publicly—but exactly 1,000 days after he resigned in 1974, he told TV interviewer David Frost, "I let the American people down.

I'll . . . carry the burden the rest of my life." In 1998 Bill Clinton took responsibility for his affair with White House intern Monica Lewinsky 212 days after it was alleged. In 2005 George W. Bush took responsibility for the government's response to Hurricane Katrina fifteen days after the storm made landfall. In 1961 John Kennedy took responsibility for the failed Bay of Pigs invasion six days later, and in 1980 it took Jimmy Carter one day to take the blame for the failed attempt to rescue the hostages in Iran. **What you can do:** If you want to apologize effectively: (1) make it genuine; (2) do it promptly; (3) don't justify your bad behavior during the apology; (4) make a commitment to not do again what you did wrong; and (5) be prepared for anything, including indifference or a rejected apology.

AS GOVERNOR OF TEXAS AND AS PRESIDENT, GEORGE W. BUSH RAILED AGAINST FRIVOLOUS LAWSUITS, SO WHAT'S THIS ABOUT BUSH SUING A RENTAL CAR COMPANY OVER A FENDER BENDER?
On September 8, 1998, while he was governor, one of Bush's twin daughters was driving his 1995 Jeep when she was involved in an accident with a driver who was driving a rental car with a suspended license. No one was injured, but Bush sued Enterprise Rent-A-Car, claiming that the company shared the blame for renting a vehicle to someone with a suspended license. Bush received $2,500 in a settlement.

CLIMATE CHANGE HAS BECOME A FRONT-BURNER ENVIRONMENTAL—AND POLITICAL—ISSUE. PROOF OF THE POLITICAL PART IS THE NUMBER OF LOBBYISTS KNOCKING ON CONGRESSMEN'S DOORS IN WASHINGTON. HOW MANY ARE THERE?
More than 2,800—about 2,300 more than in 2003. Of that total, 2,349 represent industries that oppose regulations to curb global warming, about 300 come from industries that favor regulations, and the remainder claim to be neutral about potential regulations. In all, there are nearly five climate lobbyists for every member of Congress. **What you can**

do: Want to learn more about climate change and global warming? There are thousands of sources of information. Make sure you understand who funds the source you trust.

MOST PEOPLE WOULD GUESS—AND THEY'D GUESS RIGHT—THAT NEVADA HAS THE HIGHEST DIVORCE RATE IN THE UNITED STATES. WHICH HAS THE LOWEST?

Washington, DC's rate is 2.1 per 1,000 people. A theory: Lots of young, single people move there to work for the government but don't marry until after they move away. If you think DC shouldn't count because it's not a state, Pennsylvania is lowest, with a rate of 2.2. Nevada's divorce rate, by the way, is 6.7 per 1,000 people. **Bonus question: The American Association for Marriage and Family Therapy had thirty-five members when it was founded in 1942. How many does it have today?** About 24,000.

REPUBLICAN CANDIDATES—AT LEAST AT THE FEDERAL LEVEL—HAVE TALKED UP CONSERVATIVE FAMILY VALUES MORE THAN DEMOCRATS. IS THERE ANYTHING BEHIND THAT TALK?

Not really. Look at the 2008 presidential election between President Barack Obama, a Democrat, and Republican John McCain: Of the ten states with the highest divorce rates, eight voted for McCain. Of the ten states with the highest teenage birthrates, eight voted for McCain. Of the ten states with the highest rate of subscriptions to pornographic sites, eight voted for McCain. Oklahoma, which is in the top ten for highest divorce rates, highest teenage birthrates, and most porn subscriptions, has seventy-seven counties, all of which voted for McCain.

WHAT PERCENTAGE OF AMERICANS FAVORS ALLOWING "HOMOSEXUALS" TO SERVE IN THE MILITARY, AND WHAT PERCENTAGE THINKS "GAY MEN AND LESBIANS" SHOULD BE ABLE TO SERVE?

Sometimes our choice of words means different things to different people. Seventy percent say they are comfortable with "gay men and lesbians" serving, but only 59 percent are OK with "homosexuals" in the military, according to a recent poll. Twenty-nine percent somewhat oppose or strongly oppose "homosexuals" serving while only 19 percent somewhat oppose or strongly oppose "gay men and lesbians" in the military.

IS IT TRUE THAT HUSBANDS AND WIVES WHO SPEND MORE TIME SCRUBBING THE FLOORS AND DOING THE LAUNDRY TOGETHER CARVE OUT LESS TIME TO SNUGGLE IN THE BEDROOM?

Apparently not. A recent study of 6,877 couples shows that husbands and wives who spend time doing household chores together are having more sex. The study contradicts other studies—and the long-held belief—that couples have less time for sex if they're spending more time working around the house. But some couples say hard work gives them more energy to play hard, and others say doing housework together strengthens their bond and gives them a greater appreciation for their partners, leading to a greater desire for intimacy. **What you can do:** Wash dishes, mop the floor, scrub the tub, do windows, dust something, etc., etc. ☺

WHAT PERCENTAGE OF MARRIAGES SURVIVES INFIDELITY?

It depends who's cheating. About 75 percent of marriages survive if the male is cheating, and about 65 percent survive if the female is having the affair. Marriages in which males cheat are more likely to survive, therapists say, because men are less likely than women to have an emotional attachment with their mistresses. Without that attachment, couples can more easily address the underlying issues that triggered the cheating and save their marriages. And in some cases, the marriages actually improve. **Bonus question: What percentage survives cancer?** Again, it depends who has it. In a five-year study involving more than 500 people, the stress associated with a cancer diagnosis led to a separation or divorce 2.9 percent of the time if the husband was diagnosed, and it led to a separation or divorce

20.8 percent of the time if the wife had cancer. The researchers theorize that wives are more supportive than husbands when times get tough. Couples who were married the longest were more likely to stay together. **What you can do:** Seek counseling even if you think your marriage is doing well.

WHAT PERCENTAGE OF AMERICANS SAID THEY WOULD ACT IMMORALLY TO KEEP THEIR JOBS?

Twenty-eight. That response came in a survey in February 2009, three months after a recession was declared in the United States.

WHAT PERCENTAGE OF AMERICAN MEN AGES EIGHTEEN TO TWENTY-NINE BELIEVE THAT STANDING UP DURING SEX WILL PREVENT PREGNANCY?

Eighteen. These sorts of beliefs are at least partially responsible for the rates of unplanned pregnancies. Half of all pregnancies in the United States are unplanned. Among people ages twenty to twenty-nine, three out of five pregnancies are unplanned. Three out of ten girls are pregnant before they turn twenty, and six out of ten teens who engage in sex say they wish they had waited.

WHAT PERCENTAGE OF ENGLISH WOMEN SAY THEY'VE NEVER—NOT ONCE—HAD SEX WHILE SOBER?

Six. British women drink alcohol before having sex because they lack confidence in their bodies, according to researchers who interviewed a random sampling of 3,000 women. The women said alcohol loosened them up, and 75 percent of women said they even liked a drink or two before getting into bed with their husbands or boyfriends. The study also found that the average woman has had sex with eight men and was drunk with at least five of them—so drunk that they couldn't remember the names of two of them. And nine out of ten women said they would never date without drinking.

SPEAKING OF BIRDS, WHAT'S THE MOST PROMISCUOUS BIRD IN THE WORLD?

The salt-marsh sparrow, a small, stocky bird found from Maine to North Carolina, really gets around. Most small birds are believed to be monogamous, but Connecticut-based researchers found that at least 97 percent of female salt-marsh sparrows were mating with more than one male. Only the greater vasa parrot of Madagascar and the superb fairy-wren of Australia are known to come close to the salt-marsh sparrow. Using fine mesh nets, the researchers caught adult females and males and chicks, then banded them and took blood samples to test the birds' DNA. The researchers discovered that there was only a 23 percent chance that two chicks in the same nest had the same father.

FELLATIO HAS BEEN THOUGHT TO BE THE SOLE DOMAIN OF HUMANS AND BONOBO CHIMPANZEES, BUT SCIENTISTS RECENTLY DISCOVERED THAT ANOTHER SPECIES LIKES TO DO IT. WHAT IS IT?

Turns out about seven out of ten female short-nosed fruit bats perform fellatio on their mates, and it has this added benefit: Intercourse lasts about four minutes for fellators—twice as long as for females that don't do it. On average, for every second of fellatio, intercourse lasts an additional six seconds. Why do some short-nosed fruit bats like sex to last longer? Well, we can only speculate, of course. Researchers say it certainly would keep rival female bats away longer, and it also could help move sperm. And it just might feel good, but fruit bats don't kiss and tell.

MOST MALE BEDBUGS THAT WANT TO HAVE SEX ARE NOT THE LEAST BIT PARTICULAR ABOUT THEIR PARTNERS—MALE, FEMALE, THEY DON'T CARE. WHAT HAVE RESEARCHERS DISCOVERED ABOUT MALE BEDBUGS THAT AREN'T IN THE MOOD TO HAVE SEX WITH OTHER MALES?

They emit an antipredator pheromone that tells frisky males to stay away. A bedbug's penis is like a needle, and females have a way to guide it so it doesn't pierce the abdomen, as sometimes happens during homosexual sex. This is the first time scientists have seen bedbugs use their pheromone for sexual purposes. Males use it more often to ward off violent attacks that don't involve sexual assaults.

IN CHICAGO, WHAT'S MORE LIKELY TO HAPPEN—THAT A PROSTITUTE WILL HAVE SEX FOR FREE WITH A POLICE OFFICER OR THAT A POLICE OFFICER WILL ARREST HER FOR PROSTITUTION?
The former. There's a 3 percent chance that a prostitute will give a "freebie" to a police officer and a 1.5 percent chance that a police officer will arrest her. The study that arrived at this conclusion also stated that prostitutes who work with pimps are less likely to be arrested and that prostitutes earn about $27 an hour. But they don't work anything close to forty hours a week, so that hourly wage amounts to less than $20,000 a year. To compare, a lady working a forty-hour-a-week, minimum-wage job in Illinois, where the study was conducted, would earn $17,160—without the risks of violence and sexually transmitted diseases.

Nine

HITLER LIKED BEER— AND CAKE

History isn't always easy to make fresh because, after all, it has been told many times over, right? Not always. Some of the facts in this chapter come from newly declassified documents or recent interviews or discoveries about historical figures or events. You'll find recently released information about Adolf Hitler and Saddam Hussein and an incredible, little-known link between Abraham Lincoln and the Secret Service.

KING TUT IS ARGUABLY THE WORLD'S BEST-KNOWN MUMMY BECAUSE HIS REMAINS HAVE BEEN STUDIED SO EXTENSIVELY, BUT WHAT DID SCIENTISTS ONLY RECENTLY DISCOVER ABOUT HIM?
His cause of death. King Tutankhamun, the boy pharaoh who captured the public's imagination when a British anthropologist discovered his tomb in 1922, died of malaria and a degenerative bone condition at the age of nineteen. A team of seventeen

anthropologists and medical doctors spent two years studying Tut and fifteen other royal mummies who died between 1550 BC and 1324 BC. Using the latest radiological and genetic technology, the scientists found malaria in other mummies as well. The study, which ended in October 2009, turned up no evidence of foul play related to Tut's death, as some historians have theorized. It turns out he was just sick and frail most of his brief life.

WHY ARE ARCHAEOLOGISTS SO EXCITED ABOUT THE 200 OR SO INHABITANTS OF A 4,000-YEAR-OLD CEMETERY IN A CHINESE DESERT JUST NORTH OF TIBET?

The short answer is everything about the place is just so weird. First of all, the inhabitants of the cemetery look like Europeans, with long noses and brown hair, and, in fact, they possess European and Siberian genetic markers. Chinese scientists theorize that Europeans and Siberians intermarried before they moved about 4,000 years ago to what is now China's northwest region of Xinjiang, where the extremely dry air helped preserve the bodies. If their appearance weren't odd enough, archaeologists found each well-dressed body buried under upside-down boats, which were covered by cowhides. And each boat was marked, not by a gravestone, but by a thirteen-foot-tall pole. Archaeologists noted that the poles stuck in the ground by men's bodies were carved at the top and looked like oar blades, while the poles buried by women's bodies were not carved. The archaeologists didn't know what to make of that until they found life-size wooden phalluses buried next to the women's bodies. If the phalluses represented penises, then the carved poles with the flat blades, they concluded, represented vulvas—a believable analysis, other scientists say. One last oddity: The location of the cemetery, near a dried-up river, is so inhospitable that archaeologists say the people buried there must have lived elsewhere and went to extremes to transport the bodies and the thirteen-foot-tall poles to this desolate site.

MUCH IS KNOWN ABOUT ADOLF HITLER BECAUSE MUCH HAS BEEN WRITTEN ABOUT HIM, BUT WHAT ARE SOME THINGS THAT ONLY HITLER SCHOLARS MAY KNOW?

Hitler, who didn't like direct exposure to the sun, was a night owl who usually ate dinner at 8:00 p.m., according to a British intelligence report that surfaced in 2009 when it was sold at auction. Although he often sat at the table for two hours with his generals, he ate his dinner—often vegetable stew, stewed fruit, and a glass or two of beer—in a few minutes and rarely joined in on the conversation. At the table, he bit his fingernails and had a habit of running his index finger under his nose. At midnight or 1:00 a.m., he would invite high-ranking officials to his quarters for snacks, including large amounts of cake. At 2:00 a.m., he took a walk, alone, before he went to bed. But he didn't sacrifice sleep, often waking up after 11:00 a.m.

SPEAKING OF DICTATORS, SADDAM HUSSEIN MOVED CONSTANTLY FROM PALACE TO PALACE FOR SECURITY REASONS, BUT WHAT SECURITY MEASURE SURPRISED HIS DEBRIEFERS THE MOST?

After his capture in December 2003, the Iraqi dictator told a Farsi-speaking FBI agent who he came to like that he spoke only twice on the telephone after 1990. Hussein said long-held beliefs that he employed look-alikes to confuse would-be assassins were not true.

CONSPIRACY THEORISTS WHO BELIEVE LEE HARVEY OSWALD DID NOT ACT ALONE WHEN HE KILLED PRESIDENT JOHN F. KENNEDY OFTEN POINT TO A 1963 PHOTO OF OSWALD HOLDING A RIFLE THAT THEY SAY WAS OBVIOUSLY DOCTORED. TRUE?

False. New research that measured for inconsistencies in the photo's pixels found it was not tampered with. Conspiracy theorists long insisted that shadows under Oswald's nose and behind him look like they were made by different light sources, leading them to believe that Oswald's head was placed onto another man's body in the photo. Not so, says the researcher, who added that the image would have been impossible to fake that way using 1963 technology.

THE USS *MONITOR*, THE FAMOUS CIVIL WAR IRONCLAD THAT SUNK OFF THE COAST OF NORTH CAROLINA DURING A STORM IN THE WEE HOURS OF DECEMBER 31, 1862, IS WELL-KNOWN FOR ITS FIGHT TO A DRAW WITH THE CONFEDERATE IRONCLAD THE *VIRGINIA*. WHEN ITS TURRET WAS RAISED ABOUT 145 YEARS LATER, WHAT WAS ONE OF THE STRANGEST DISCOVERIES ONBOARD?
Divers found numerous bottles of Gray's Hair Restoration, a truly odd discovery on a ship manned almost exclusively by men in their late teens and early twenties—until you know that the U.S. Navy outlawed alcohol onboard its ships only a few months before the *Monitor* sank. Naval historians confidently theorize that the crew used these hair tonic bottles to smuggle alcohol aboard.

THE UNITED STATES HAS HELD ELECTIONS ON THE FIRST TUESDAY AFTER THE FIRST MONDAY IN NOVEMBER FOR NEARLY 170 YEARS. WHY TUESDAY? WHY NOVEMBER? AND WHY NOT THE *FIRST* TUESDAY?
Back then, polling places, especially in rural areas, were spread out, and it could take a day or longer to reach your county seat to vote. If Congress chose to hold elections on Mondays, many people would have been forced to leave their homes on Sundays, which were reserved for going to church and resting. The United States was very much of an agricultural nation during the nineteenth century, and November was considered a convenient month for farmers to vote because harvesting was mostly over by then but severe winter weather hadn't yet settled in—and the earlier in the month, the less likely bad weather would inconvenience voters. So Election Day would always fall on a Tuesday and always a Tuesday in early November, but Congress knew November 1 was out of the question. Not only is November 1 All Saints Day, a holy day in the Roman Catholic

Church, but many merchants back then did their books on the first of each month. The first Tuesday of the month could fall on November 1, so the first Tuesday after the first Monday was chosen, leaving open the possibility that Election Day could occur as early as November 2 and as late as November 8.

WHAT DIDN'T YOU LEARN ABOUT OUR FOUNDING FATHERS IN SCHOOL THAT WOULD HAVE MADE AMERICAN HISTORY CLASS A LOT MORE INTERESTING?

George Washington never had wooden teeth—his lower denture was carved from hippopotamus ivory—but he did, in fact, lose nearly all of his teeth by the time he became president. Washington would stuff his cheeks with cotton when he posed for portraits to keep his face from looking sunken. He was also the only founding father who never attended college, and he avoided physical contact so rigorously that in public he often held his hat with one hand and gripped his sword with the other in order to keep from shaking hands with anyone. (Instead, he preferred bowing.) Washington, who was well-known as a gentleman farmer, is much less known as a bootlegger. In 1798, his distillery produced more than 11,000 gallons of alcohol, the largest output in America at the time. **Bonus question: George Washington appointed more U.S. Supreme Court justices than any other full-term president (eleven). Who appointed the fewest?** Jimmy Carter, a one-term president, appointed none.

James Madison, at about five foot four and less than a hundred pounds, was so small that he was rejected as a Revolutionary War soldier and most of his life was teased about his size. But he had the last laugh, marrying the charming and vivacious Dolley Madison and outliving all of the other founding fathers. He died on June 28, 1836, at the age of eighty-five.

Thomas Jefferson, a lawyer, diplomat, philosopher, musician, theologian, paleontologist, scientist, inventor, linguist, astronomer, statesman, and U.S. president, often preferred wearing dirty and tattered clothing and sometimes greeted dignitaries with uncombed hair and worn-out slippers. Some historians speculate that he had a type of autism called Asperger's syndrome, which could have contributed to this behavior.

Benjamin Franklin, one of three Americans to sign the peace treaty with England that ended the Revolutionary War, fathered an illegitimate son, William, who became governor of New Jersey and supported the British in the war. About 20,000 people attended Franklin's funeral on April 21, 1790, making that the largest public gathering in the nation's history up till that time, but William was not believed to be one of them.

Alexander Hamilton, who was born out of wedlock in the West Indies and moved to the colonies at seventeen, is considered to be one of George Washington's closest allies, but before Washington was elected, Hamilton joined a group of dignitaries that asked Prussia's Prince Henry to be king of America. The group changed its mind before Henry could reply.

John Adams was the first president to live in the White House, but he was only there for four months, losing the presidency to Jefferson shortly after moving in. That was fine with Adams' wife, Abigail, who often complained about the White House's unfinished state.

SPEAKING OF THE WHITE HOUSE, WHAT ELSE DON'T 99.99 PERCENT OF AMERICANS KNOW ABOUT IT?

For starters, it couldn't have been built as it was without foreigners, who had skills that no Americans possessed at the time. Scots raised its sandstone walls and carved the rose and garland ornaments and scalloped patterns on the outside walls while Italian artists carved the decorations on the porticoes. The 132-room White House, which was added on to a few times during the first half of the nineteenth century, was the largest residence in the nation until after the Civil War, when the barons of the industrial age began building their mansions. The house wasn't called the White House until Theodore Roosevelt gave his blessing to the name in 1901, and it wasn't wheelchair accessible until 1933, when Franklin D. Roosevelt needed it to be. In 1948, after it was discovered that 150 years of wear and tear and two fires had weakened its load-bearing walls, the White House was gutted and its walls reinforced with steel beams.

WHICH PRESIDENTS GAVE THE SHORTEST AND LONGEST INAUGURATION SPEECHES, AND WHAT DID THEY HAVE IN COMMON?

At 135 words, George Washington's second inaugural address was the shortest. Forty-eight years later to the day, William Henry Harrison, who chose not to wear an overcoat on a cold and wet early March day, delivered an edited-down, 8,444-word speech that took nearly two hours to read. Three weeks later, apparently unrelated to Harrison's exposure to the elements during his speech, he developed cold symptoms, then pneumonia and pleurisy, an inflammation of the lining of the cavity surrounding the lungs. He died a week later, serving the shortest ever presidential term—thirty days, twelve hours, and thirty minutes. Historians say both speeches have at least one thing in common: They were dreadfully dull. **What you can do:** Researchers say the vast majority of public speakers lose their audience's attention after the first ten minutes. So if you're speaking to a group, at least every ten minutes sprinkle in an amusing anecdote, show a photo or a video, or pull out a prop.

IS THERE ANY LINK BETWEEN PRESIDENT LINCOLN AND THE SECRET SERVICE?

Lincoln authorized the creation of the Secret Service on April 14, 1865. Does that date ring a bell? It was also the date he was shot by John Wilkes Booth. Back then, however, the Secret Service was set up only to combat counterfeit currency. It started providing full-time protection for presidents in 1901 when two agents were assigned to the White

House. Presidential candidates began receiving protection after Robert F. Kennedy was killed while campaigning in 1968.

WHAT DON'T MOST AMERICANS KNOW ABOUT THE CONSTITUTION?

A lot, but here are three tidbits that even many history buffs don't know: (1) the four-page, 4,440-word document does not include the word "democracy"; (2) the clerk who handwrote it in 1787 was paid the handsome sum of $30—about $400 today—but he apparently could have used spell-check; the Constitution contains a bunch of misspelled words, most glaringly "Pensylvania," just above the signers' names; and (3) in order to preserve it, the four glass cases where it is kept are filled with argon gas and kept at 67 degrees and 40 percent humidity. **What you can do:** The Constitution is on display in the National Archives Building in Washington, DC. The building is open from 10:00 a.m. to 7:00 p.m. from March 15 to Labor Day and from 10:00 a.m. to 5:30 p.m. from the day after Labor Day to March 14. It's closed only two days a year—Thanksgiving and Christmas. Like the other public museums in Washington, DC, there is no charge to enter the building or see the Constitution.

Ten

THE LEFTOVER BUT EQUALLY FASCINATING STUFF

This chapter is for all of the stuff—literature, art, education, and more—that didn't fit elsewhere, but these facts are far from castaways. What will you learn in this final section? What's got twenty-six kitchens, twenty-four restaurants, twenty-one swimming pools, eighteen window-washing robots, one jail, and one helicopter landing pad? Who watches the most TV? Who's better at detecting body odor—men or women? Where do the best, worst, and fastest drivers live, and if we're bad drivers, can we blame that on our parents? In this chapter, readers will also learn where the Garden of Eden was located, why Russia was better off as a Communist nation, and why anthropologists are fascinated with a tribe of hunters and gatherers in Tanzania.

ON A SCALE OF 1 TO 10, WITH 1 BEING NOT ANNOYED AND 10 BEING "ANNOYS YOU TREMEN-DOUSLY," WHAT BUGS AMERICANS THE MOST?

Hidden fees scored an 8.9 overall in a survey of 1,125 adults. With a score of 8.6, not getting a person on the phone came in second, followed by tailgating (8.3), drivers talking on cell phones (8.0), incomprehensible bills (7.8), and dog poop left on the ground (7.6). In all, the survey takers were asked about twenty-one annoying things. Last place? Inaccurate weather forecasts, which scored only 4.3. **What you can do:** One somewhat controversial tip to deal with daily annoyances: Lower your expectations. If you expect drivers to be considerate and proficient, then tailgating will bother you more. That's why a blown weather forecast bothers us least. We don't really expect our weather forecasters to get it right very often, so when they don't, we're generally OK with it.

WHAT PERCENTAGE OF AMERICAN WORKERS ARE SATISFIED WITH THEIR JOBS, AND WHAT ARE SOME COMPANIES DOING ABOUT IT?

Only 45 percent. And that's down from 52 percent in 2005 and 61 percent in 1987, according to a group that surveys 5,000 households a year. In fact, 45 percent is the lowest satisfaction rate in the twenty-two years that the survey has been done. Numerous studies show that happy workers are more productive, so to combat this dissatisfaction, some companies, including KPMG, American Express, and UBS, are hiring happiness coaches—yes, they're called happiness coaches—who work with employees to help them control their moods and adopt a positive attitude. **Bonus question: What's happening in France?** A company called France Telecom, hoping to improve morale in the wake of a rash of suicides, decided to determine senior managers' bonuses based on the happiness of rank-and-file workers and other social factors. **What you can do:** If you feel the need, try some of the things that the happiness coaches teach: (1) meditate daily; (2) write down what you're thankful for; (3) thank your coworkers for something they've done; and (4) find a positive in what seems like a negative situation.

WHICH NATION'S WORKERS GET THE MOST VACATION TIME?

It's a tie between two very different places: Brazil and Lithuania, where workers receive at least forty-one paid days off a year. In Brazil, the minimum number of vacation days workers can legally receive is thirty, and in Lithuania it's twenty-eight, but workers in Lithuania receive thirteen paid public holidays, two more than workers in Brazil. Other nations where workers benefit from generous leave policies include Russia (at least forty days), Austria (thirty-eight), and Poland and the United Kingdom (both thirty-six). The United States is one of the only countries that don't require companies to give employees a minimum number of vacation days per year, though the average is about fifteen, with most workers also receiving between six and ten paid public holidays. Canadian and Chinese workers get the worst deals, receiving an average of only twenty paid days off a year. **Bonus question: Which nation's workers use the fewest numbers of allotted vacation days?** South Korea. In 2009 government workers took an average of only six of the twenty-three vacation days they were given, according to a survey. The country's president, Lee Myung-bak, takes about two vacation days a year. **What you can do:** Want to negotiate better vacation leave for yourself? The two best times to do it are when you're offered the job and when you tell your supervisor about an offer from another company. Always ask for more vacation than you think you'll get, but be reasonable. Don't ask for eight weeks of vacation if you have reason to believe that no one at the firm gets more than four weeks.

WHAT PERCENTAGE OF EMPLOYERS SAYS THEY EXPECT VACATIONING WORKERS TO CHECK IN WITH THE OFFICE?

Forty-nine. And 25 percent of all workers say they expect to call the office at least once while they're on vacation. This is according to a 2010 survey involving more than 2,800 workers. **What you can do:** To ensure your vacation is a true break from work: (1) schedule your vacation at a time when few of your colleagues are gone so your office isn't too shorthanded while you're away; (2) train a coworker to do what you do to ensure that someone at your office can do your job; and (3) if you're a supervisor, don't call the office while you're gone, so other workers will not feel pressured to do so during their vacations.

WHAT'S THE MOST COMMON COMPUTER PASSWORD, AND IF YOU USE IT, WHY SHOULD YOU PUT DOWN THIS BOOK RIGHT NOW AND CHANGE IT?

It's 123456. Nearly 1 percent of all computer users picked that one, according to a survey that examined 32 million passwords stolen by a hacker from a company that makes software for users of social networking sites. The next most popular password was 12345, followed by 123456789, password, iloveyou, princess, rockyou, 1234567, 12345678, and abc123. Twenty percent of the users chose passwords from a pool of 5,000. Computer security experts say if you have one of these passwords, you're making it easy for a hacker to steal your identity, your information, and your money. **What you can do:** Most hackers make educated assumptions when going about their work, so make it difficult for them by selecting passwords no one would guess. Start by choosing the longest password possible—at least twelve characters—and include numerals, preferably sprinkled in between letters. **Bonus question: Which country has the fastest Internet?** South Korea, at 11 megabytes per second, is the fastest, followed by Japan (8.0), Hong Kong (7.6), Sweden (6.9), and Romania (6.2). The United States comes in at 4.2 and Canada at 3.8.

WHEN IT COMES TO PASSING ALONG MALWARE, WHICH COUNTRIES' DOMAINS ARE THE MOST AND LEAST DANGEROUS?

The central African nation of Cameroon (.cm) is the riskiest. Nearly 37 percent of the sites with the .cm domain pose a security risk, a computer security firm found. The next riskiest are China (.cn) at 23.4 percent, Samoa (.ws) at 17.8 percent, and the Philippines (.ph) at 13.1 percent. The safest? Only .1 percent of the sites in Japan (.jp), Ireland (.ie), Croatia (.hr), and Luxembourg (.lu) posed a risk. It turns out the world's most popular domain, .com, is the second riskiest overall at 32.2 percent while .gov is the safest (0 percent). Which brings us back to Cameroon. The domain .cm is a common typo for .com, so cybercriminals use the .cm domain to create fake websites that churn out malicious downloads and other unwanted programs.

WHICH COUNTRY'S HACKERS MOST WORRY THE INFORMATION TECHNOLOGY EXECUTIVES CHARGED WITH PROTECTING THEIR COMPANIES FROM CYBERATTACKS?

The United States. Thirty-six percent of IT executives in a global survey identified the United States as the greatest concern, followed by China (33 percent), Russia (12 percent), the United Kingdom (5 percent), and France and Germany (both 2 percent).

DOES ANYONE REALLY READ SPAM E-MAIL?

Yes, believe it or not, and some people actually buy things from spam e-mail solicitations. As part of a study conducted in 2008, nearly 348 million e-mail messages touting pharmaceutical products were sent over twenty-six days, resulting in twenty-eight sales, twenty-seven of which involved male enhancement products. That figures to a success rate of 0.00001 percent. (Of those 348 million e-mail messages, spam blockers prevented all but 82.7 million e-mails from reaching their destinations.) Some might say a success rate of 0.0001 is pretty lousy, but many spam solicitors say they can make money with a success rate of 0.000001.

DOES THE BACKGROUND COLOR OF YOUR COMPUTER SCREEN HELP YOU PERFORM TASKS OR WRITE BETTER?

Researchers at British Columbia University think so. They gave 600 people tasks at computers with different color backgrounds. Those with red backgrounds performed better on tests of recall while those with blue backgrounds did better on tests that required creativity. The researchers said the results are not tied solely to computer screens. People will be more accurate if they work in rooms with red walls, and more creative in rooms with blue walls. The experts say colors may influence how we do on tests because of the moods they create. **What you can do:** If your eyes ache when you use the computer, make an appointment with an eye doctor to see if you need glasses or a new prescription. Short of that, take frequent breaks from the computer to relax your eyes. Make sure that the room where your computer is located is well lit and that there is no glare.

THE AVERAGE HOME BUYER SEES TEN TO TWELVE PROPERTIES BEFORE DECIDING ON A HOUSE. WHAT'S THE MOST ANYONE HAS SEEN BEFORE BUYING?

There is no way to know for sure, but consider the house-hunting efforts made by Lidia Pringle, a Californian who visited 298 houses in Marin County, near San Francisco, from 2007 to 2009 before she found her home. Pringle, a former reporter who prides herself on being thorough in all she does, was looking for a large house with a lot of light that had two home offices, one for her and the other for her husband. They ended up with a salmon-colored Tuscan-style house that they got for $5.9 million—down from the original price of $9 million. **Bonus question: How long do most people spend looking for a house to buy?** An average of ten weeks during buyers' markets, when more houses are available and there are fewer buyers, and eight weeks during sellers' markets, when fewer houses are available and buyers feel more pressure to act. **What you can do:** Take your time. Never, ever, rush when it comes to buying a house. Real estate agents say most people who do—and especially those who participate in a bidding war with another buyer—regret it.

WHICH ARE THE HAPPIEST AND SADDEST STATES IN THE NATION?

The happiest: Louisiana, followed by, in this order, Hawaii, Florida, Tennessee, Arizona, Mississippi, Montana, South Carolina, Alabama, and Maine. The saddest: New York, then Connecticut, New Jersey, Michigan, Indiana, California, Illinois, Ohio, Massachusetts, and Rhode Island. The researchers who arrived at this conclusion blended the results of two surveys, one of which asked 1.3 million Americans about their health and their overall satisfaction with their lives, the other of which examined more objective, quality-of-life measures, such as weather, air quality, commuting time, crime, student-teacher ratios, and taxes. The researchers found a strong correlation between the surveys' subjective and objective results. **Another point worth noting:** With the exception of Ohio, Michigan, and Indiana, which have endured tough economic times, the people in the saddest states have among the highest incomes in the nation while those in the happiest states make less money than most.

WHO ARE THE WORST DRIVERS—TEENAGE BOYS OR TEENAGE GIRLS?

Girls. More girls than boys admit to speeding, driving aggressively, and fiddling with the radio, talking on the phone, or texting while driving, according to a 2009 survey of 1,063 teens done by the Allstate Foundation. Two out of three teenage boys in the survey said they would speak up if someone was driving unsafely while only about half of the girls said they would. Allstate acknowledges that girls might be more forthcoming than boys, and they say they won't use this information to set rates. Rather, they plan to use it to promote safe driving. **Bonus question: Where do the most and least knowledgeable drivers in America live?** The most knowledgeable live in Oregon and the least in New

Jersey, according to an insurance company survey of 5,000 licensed drivers, each of whom took a twenty-question test. After Oregon, the next most knowledgeable drivers live in Washington State, Iowa, and Idaho, and the least knowledgeable after New Jersey live in Washington, DC, Rhode Island, and Massachusetts. **What you can do:** For starters, learn how to merge into traffic, and use your blinker lights when changing lanes. Half of all drivers admit they don't know the proper way to merge into heavy traffic, and six out of ten drivers say they change lanes without using their blinker lights, according to the survey.

IF YOU'RE A LOUSY DRIVER, CAN YOU BLAME IT ON YOUR PARENTS?

Why not? A study found that people with a mutant gene did on average 20 percent worse on a driving test—and that 30 percent of Americans have the gene, which could explain a lot. The researchers didn't set out to prove anything about driving specifically, but they needed to have the study's participants—twenty-two people without the gene variant and seven with it—perform a skill common to everyone, and they settled on driving. The participants had to drive fifteen laps on a simulator and then return in a week and do it again. Those with the mutant gene, which controls a protein that affects memory, consistently did worse than those without it.

WHERE DO THE FASTEST AND SLOWEST HIGHWAY DRIVERS LIVE?

The fastest live in Mississippi and the slowest in Washington, DC, according to a company that compiled information from GPS devices. Those in Mississippi drive an average of 70.1 mph on the highway while DC drivers chug along at only 46.4 mph due to congested road conditions. If you want to throw out DC because it's not a state, Hawaiians drive the slowest on the highway, at 52.7 mph. Other states that average slower than 63.8 mph are Delaware, Rhode Island, Oregon, Washington, Maine, New Jersey,

Illinois, Maryland, and Massachusetts. States where highway drivers travel on average 68.5 mph or more include South Carolina, Alabama, Arkansas, Kansas, New Mexico, Arizona, Utah, Nevada, and Idaho. The caveat here is that the company that did the survey collected data from DC and only forty-five states—but not Alaska, Montana, Wyoming, or the Dakotas, some states where drivers have a reputation for driving fast on lonely rural highways.

WHAT WAS THE WORST CAR EVER BUILT, AND WHY DOES IT DESERVE THAT DISTINCTION?

The Yugo, which *Fortune* magazine listed as one of its "outstanding products of 1985," had a pretty good American debut, selling more than 1,005 cars in one day in August of 1985. At a base price of $3,990, the Yugoslavian-made car sold for much less than any American-made car, but it didn't take long for consumers to see why. For one thing, it was made in a Serbian factory that had previously made hand grenades and wasn't designed to make cars, and the workforce was encouraged to drink plum brandy throughout the day. Some Yugos rolled off the assembly line with rust spots, and a car bought by *Motor Trend* broke down during a road test. *Consumer Reports* wrote, "The clutch chattered. The brakes squealed. The speedometer clicked. The hood became loose." **What you can do:** Car dealers warn consumers about buying cars made in countries that don't have a good track record for doing so. They also urge consumers to read consumer magazines to learn about the cars they might buy before they buy them.

IS THE SIXTY-FOUR PACK OF CRAYOLA CRAYONS GOING TO SIXTY-FIVE?

Maybe. Scientists at Oregon State University in 2009 accidentally discovered a new shade of blue. They were mixing chemicals and heating them at 2,000 degrees and when a graduate student pulled heated mixed chemicals out of the furnace, they were bright blue—a unique pigment, it turns out. The student was heating manganese oxide, which is black, along with white yttrium oxide and pale yellow indium oxide. In that heat, the manganese ions absorbed red and green wavelengths of light and reflected only blue. Indium happens to be very expensive, so the scientists are looking for a cheaper alternative. No word yet on what they'll name the color.

THE DEBATE OVER THE WISDOM—AND EFFECTS—OF SPANKING WILL PROBABLY NEVER END, BUT IS IT GROWING OR DECLINING IN POPULARITY?

If we're to believe recent studies, it's becoming less popular. According to a recent survey of 962 American parents who had a child aged nineteen to thirty-five months, 2 percent of the parents said they spanked often, 24 percent spanked sometimes, and 73 percent spanked rarely or never. A 2000 survey of 3,000 parents reported that 61 percent said it's OK to spank regularly. **What you can do:** Behavioral scientists say most parents who spank do so when they're angry, and some later regret doing it. If that's you, leave the room briefly when you have the urge to spank your child, or count to ten slowly.

HOW MUCH PLASTIC WRAP DO AMERICANS BUY PER YEAR?

Enough to cover the entire state of Texas—all 268,601 square miles of it. What about wrapping paper? If every American family saved the paper from just three gifts, the re-used paper could cover 50,000 football fields.

AUTHORITIES ARE DISCOVERING MORE AND MORE MARIJUANA FARMS IN NATIONAL FORESTS. WHO'S TO BLAME?

Authorities blame Mexican drug gangs that have decided to cut down on travel costs by growing pot in U.S. national forests rather than in Mexico. Not only are they closer to their customers, but they also don't have to risk getting caught by U.S. Customs agents at the Mexican border. In 2009, authorities found pot farms in sixty-one national forests spanning sixteen states from coast to coast—an increase from forty-nine forests in ten states in 2008.

WHAT PERCENTAGE OF POKER PLAYERS REPORTED USING DRUGS AND OTHER SUBSTANCES TO IMPROVE THEIR PLAY?

Eighty. About 73 percent said they used drugs and other substances to focus and concentrate better. Others said they took drugs and other things to calm their nerves, stay awake, and improve memory. While some players—professional and amateur—reported using cocaine, marijuana, and amphetamines, many used prescription medications, as well as caffeine and energy drinks. Most of the players live in the United States and Canada, and most are males in their twenties.

IS THERE ANYTHING TO LUCKY CHARMS?

Apparently so. In one study, participants were told to study eight letters on a page and come up with as many words as they could from those letters. A group that was allowed to hold their lucky charms set higher goals and tried longer than those in a group who could not hold their lucky charms. In another study, those who could hold their lucky charms while playing a memory game did better and said they felt more capable. And in yet another study, golfers who were handed what was described as a lucky ball were 35 percent more likely to make the putt than those who were handed a ball without comment.

IS THERE A COUNTRY THAT CARES ABOUT WORLD RECORDS MORE THAN ANY OTHER?

Hard to say for sure, but here's a vote for Mexico, which has made the largest flour taco (1,654 pounds), assembled the largest groups of "Thriller" dancers (12,937), mariachi musicians (549), and kissers (about 40,000), set up the longest fashion show catwalk (4,332 feet and 2 inches), made the largest meatball (109 pounds), and cooked a two-ton cheesecake, which fed 20,000 people. For the record, Guinness says the largest number of records come from the United States.

WHERE WOULD YOU END UP IF YOU DUG A HOLE IN YOUR BACKYARD AND KEPT DIGGING UNTIL YOU REACHED THE OTHER END OF THE WORLD?

It wouldn't be China, as American children have been led to believe. More like the Indian Ocean. And Chinese diggers would end up in Chile, Argentina, or the Pacific Ocean. Bermudans would pop up in western Australia, Hawaiians in Botswana, New Zealanders in Spain, Colombians in Indonesia, and Paraguayans in Taiwan. These places on the opposite sides of the world are called antipodes.

NORTH KOREA, THE WORLD'S MOST CLOSED NATION, HASN'T RELEASED REVEALING INFORMATION ABOUT ITS ECONOMY FOR FIFTY YEARS AND HASN'T SHARED MEANINGFUL DEMOGRAPHIC DATA SINCE 1993. WHAT NEW AND SURPRISING INFORMATION ABOUT THAT COUNTRY WAS RECENTLY RELEASED?

The vast majority of North Koreans are poor. Most people live in a house that's 540 to 800 square feet, and only 58 percent of the residences have flush toilets. Half the nation's factories are closed, and severe food shortages have led to reports of starvation. Life expectancy may be rising throughout much of the world but not in North Korea, where it has decreased from about seventy-three years in 1993 to about sixty-nine years in 2008, according to the nation's latest census. And North Korean women live about seven years longer than men, exceeding the world average of 4.4 years. Farming provides the most employment there—3.4 million people are farmers—and most of the farmers are women. The second-largest occupation, government workers and soldiers, accounts for 699,000 people, disproving the nation's longtime claim of a "million-man army." **What you can do:** If you want to learn more about North Korea, check out a website called North Korean Economy Watch.

**HOW MANY LANGUAGES ARE SPOKEN IN THE WORLD TODAY, AND WHICH ARE THE MOST ENDAN-
GERED?**

Between 6,000 and 7,000. And hundreds, if not more, are endangered. One person is
known to speak Pazeh (originally spoken in Taiwan and the Philippines) and Uru and
Taushiro (central South America). Two individuals speak Vilela (southern South America) and Tinigua (northern South America), and three speak Wichita (Oklahoma). Lin-
guists are at work trying to record and preserve these and hundreds of other languages
around the world that are spoken by relatively few people. In 2010, the Bo language in
India became extinct when the last known speaker, a widow with no children, died of
old age at eighty-five. **Bonus question: What's the world's most popular language?** Mandarin Chinese, spoken by 873 million people. The number of Chinese speakers is growing in the
United States, where Chinese language classes in schools increased by 4 percent from
1997 to 2008—at a time when thousands of elementary and middle schools cut foreign
language classes. In advanced placement classes taken by high school students, Chinese
ranks third most popular, behind only Spanish and French. **What you can do:** Mandarin
and other Chinese languages are considered especially difficult to learn because many
of the words are hard to pronounce, and if you get the sounds and tones wrong, the
words can have totally different meanings. Many nonnative Mandarin and Cantonese
speakers suggest first learning the spoken language, for which you'll need to find a patient teacher who will work with you for several months or longer.

WHERE ON EARTH WAS THE GARDEN OF EDEN?

Well, that depends on who you ask, but the largest ever genetic survey of Africans,
published in 2009, suggests that southwest Africa, specifically near the Kalahari Desert where Angola and Namibia come together, is the place where modern humans first
lived, about 50,000 years ago. The researchers arrived at this conclusion after studying

121 African populations, four African American populations, and sixty non-African populations. The area they pinpointed is sandy and not exactly gardenlike. This finding is at odds with what many Christians and others believe, which is that humans first lived near where the Tigris and Euphrates rivers meet, in southern Iraq.

THE HADZAS, A TRIBE IN NORTHERN TANZANIA, FASCINATES ANTHROPOLOGISTS. WHY?

The Hadzas—hunter-gatherers who grow no food, raise no livestock, own almost nothing, and follow almost no rules—are living like their ancestors did thousands of years ago, in the days before the advent of agriculture. Ironically, farms around them are expanding, crowding the Hadzas onto about 1,000 square miles, a quarter of the land on which they once lived.

WHAT PERCENTAGE OF AFRICANS LIVE WITHOUT ELECTRICITY?

Seventy-four. A company called Lebone Solutions wants to help teach millions of Africans to make a simple fuel cell that uses bacteria in soil, manure, and other readily available materials to create enough energy to power a lamp or cell phone. They call these dirt-powered batteries. **What you can do:** If you want to learn more about this and other projects, go to Lebone's website and sign up for its newsletter.

WHICH COUNTRIES, BY PERCENTAGE, HAVE THE SMALLEST NUMBER OF PEOPLE WITH ACCESS TO MODERN WATER SOURCES?

Only 22 percent of Afghans, 29 percent of Somalis, and 40 percent of those in Papua New Guinea. This is as of 2006, the year for which the most recent data is available. **Bonus question: How much water does the average American family use to wash clothes over the course of one year?** It depends on who you want to believe. The Energy Department estimates that the average family does 400 loads of laundry a year, and each load uses 45 to 55 gallons of water—or 20,000 gallons a year. Whirlpool Corp., which makes washing machines, says about 450 loads a year—or 22,500 gallons. And Procter & Gamble Co., which sells laundry soap, says it's more like 600 loads a year—or 30,000 gallons. **What you can do:** Buy an energy-efficient washing machine, which uses only 18 to 25 gallons per load.

HOW FAR DO WOMEN IN DEVELOPING NATIONS WALK PER DAY TO FETCH WATER FOR THEIR FAMILIES?

On average, 3.7 miles. In northern Kenya, where drought is common, some women and their children walk five hours a day on a round-trip journey to bring home murky water. There's a one in eight chance that someone in the world lacks adequate drinking water because of socioeconomic conditions, but progress is being made to change this grim reality. For example, in African nations and other developing countries, as many as 4 million people are trying a very simple and effective method of water purification: They take clear plastic bottles, tear off any labels, fill them with untreated water and seal the bottles with their caps. Then they lay the bottles in the sun on a sheet of metal. In six hours, the sun's UV rays kill viruses, parasites, and bacteria in the water so it can be drunk. **What you can do:** The vast majority of Americans have plenty of clean water to use, but that doesn't mean we should waste it. To conserve water: (1) never pour water down the drain when there may be another use for it (for example, use it to water your indoor plants or garden); (2) repair dripping faucets by replacing washers—one drop per second wastes 2,700 gallons of water per year; (3) choose appliances that use less water; (4) plant drought-tolerant grass, shrubs, and trees; (5) use mulch to retain moisture in the soil; and (6) use barrels or underground tanks to collect water that runs off your roof.

THE COLLAPSE OF THE SOVIET UNION IN 1991 WAS SEEN AS A LIBERATING EXPERIENCE FOR ITS PEOPLE, BUT WAS RUSSIA BETTER OFF AS A COMMUNIST NATION?

That debate won't be settled here, but here's an argument that it's not better off now: Russia has 5 million fewer people but more crime, more people diagnosed with disease, fewer hospitals and cinemas, and less farmland than it did before 1991. Russians divorce more than they did before the collapse, drink more alcohol, and live shorter lives.

WHICH COUNTRIES ARE GROWING THE FASTEST, AND WHICH ARE LOSING THEIR POPULATION THE FASTEST?

The African nations of Uganda, Niger, and Burundi are expected to grow at a rate of 263 percent, 261 percent, and 220 percent, respectively, between 2008 and 2050, while Bulgaria and Swaziland are expected to lose 35 percent and 33 percent of their population during that period, and the former Soviet Union nations of Georgia and Ukraine are each expected to lose 28 percent. The United States' population, by the way, is expected to grow by 44 percent by 2050.

WHICH COUNTRIES LIVE IN THE MOST AND LEAST CROWDED CONDITIONS?

In Monaco, an average of 34,000 people live in every square kilometer, followed by Macao (21,192) and Singapore (7,013). The least-crowded places are French Guiana, Mongolia, and Western Sahara, where there are two people per square kilometer. In Australia and Canada, there are three people per square kilometer, and in the United States, there are thirty-two.

WHICH U.S. STATE RETAINS MOST OF ITS ADULTS, AND WHICH RETAINS THE FEWEST?

Nearly 76 percent of the adults who live in Texas were born there, followed by North Carolina (71 percent), Georgia (70 percent), and California and Wisconsin (both 69 percent). Only 13 percent of the adults who live in Washington, DC, were born there. Throw out the District, and the state in last place is Alaska, at 28 percent.

WHICH STATE ATTRACTS THE MOST ADULTS, AND WHICH ATTRACTS THE FEWEST?
Eighty-six percent of the adults in Nevada weren't born there, followed by Arizona (72 percent) and Alaska (71 percent). Only 19 percent of the adults in New York and 20 percent in Louisiana were born elsewhere.

THREE U.S. TOWNS CLAIM A POPULATION OF ONE, BUT NONE OF THEM WAS COUNTED FIRST IN THE 2010 CENSUS. WHICH WAS, AND WHY WAS THAT QUITE AN ACCOMPLISHMENT?
Noorvik, Alaska, population 634, in the northwest part of the state. Being first was a pretty remarkable feat, given that Census workers there often had to trudge through the elements in snowshoes or reach remote destinations in dogsleds. The 2010 form, by the way, was available in English, Spanish, Chinese, Vietnamese, Korean, and Russian, and it included ten questions, making it one of the shortest in history. The 1960 form, by contrast, included eighty-one questions.

SO MUCH ATTENTION IS GIVEN TO THE TALLEST, LONGEST, SHORTEST, MOST POPULAR AND MOST POPULATED. WHO'S IN SECOND PLACE (WITH #1 IN PARENTHESES)?
At twelve feet, the African elephant is the second-tallest animal (giraffe). Spain, which attracts about 60 million tourists a year, is the second-most-popular tourist destination (France). The New York City metropolitan area, with 19 million people, is the second-largest city (Tokyo). The 4,000-mile-long Amazon is the second-longest river (Nile). At 28,251 feet, K2, also known as Savage Mountain, is the second-highest point on Earth (Everest). The second-tallest man-made structure is KVLY-TV's 2,063-foot transmitting tower, in North Dakota (Burj Khalifa, 160 stories and 2,717 feet tall—about the height of two Empire State Buildings).

WHICH AGE GROUP WATCHES MORE TV—FOURTEEN TO TWENTY-FIVE, TWENTY-SIX TO FORTY-TWO, OR FORTY-THREE TO SIXTY-ONE?

The youngest group watches eleven hours per week; the middle group, fifteen hours; and the oldest one, nineteen hours. The theory behind this: The younger group is busier with school, the middle group with their children—but the older group has more free time.

WHO ARE THE WORLD'S DUMBEST CRIMINALS?

Although there are plenty of worthy candidates, how many can compete with the folks who stole the two-ton Henry Moore bronze statue from his estate thirty miles north of London? The still-at-large thieves, who used a crane and a flatbed truck to steal the statue, cut it up the night they took it so it could be sold for scrap. The sculpture was valued at $4.6 million in 2005. As scrap metal, it would have fetched about $2,300—before expenses.

DO BOYS WITH GOOD GROOMING HABITS DO BETTER IN SCHOOL THAN BOYS WHO DON'T CARE ABOUT TOUSLED HAIR AND DIRTY FINGERNAILS?

Yes, if you believe the results of a study by four researchers who examined a survey of more than 20,000 seventh to twelfth graders. Well-groomed boys received better grades than sloppy boys, but good grooming didn't matter as much for girls, who benefited most from a pleasant personality. The researchers theorize that the discipline that causes boys to properly groom themselves might also lead them to work harder in school and that girls with cheerful personalities might also possess positive attitudes that will help them succeed. The researchers point out that they have no direct evidence of teacher bias, but they believe it exists and that attractive students of both sexes benefit from it. **What you can do:** This research supports other similar research done in workplaces. It makes sense that we're influenced by someone's appearance. Disregard this at your peril.

DO AMERICANS APPRECIATE UNEXPECTED FREEBIES AS MUCH AS, SAY, ASIANS?

More so, it appears. In one experiment, Americans and Asians reacted the same to receiving a free cup of coffee they were told was coming, but when they received the coffee without knowing it was on the way, Americans were more pleased than were Asians. In other experiments, Asians seemed to be thrilled with gifts that came as a result of luck while Americans preferred gifts that came as a reward for hard work.

PARIS IS WIDELY CONSIDERED ONE OF THE WORLD'S MOST ROMANTIC CITIES, BUT WHAT HAS STUNK UP THAT REPUTATION?

Pipi, as the French say. Parisians are struggling with an epidemic of public urination and have formed a law enforcement brigade to catch the offenders. In 2006, Paris also installed more than 400 free, self-cleaning, public restrooms, some with skylights. Despite this, the infractions are on the rise.

WHAT'S THE WORLD'S BIGGEST CRUISE SHIP, AND WHAT DOES IT HAVE GOING FOR IT?

At 1,181 feet long and 236 feet above the water, MS *Oasis of the Seas* dwarfs other cruise ships, not to mention nuclear-powered aircraft carriers. Aboard the $1.4-billion Royal Caribbean ship, which had its maiden voyage in December 2009, are twenty-six kitchens, twenty-four restaurants, one jail, one helicopter landing pad, eighteen window-washing robots, twenty-one swimming pools, including two wave pools and a water park for kids, and a so-called Central Park with about 12,000 plants. Some 1,250 video cameras watch over the 6,296 passengers and 2,165 crew members. Its six generators produce enough electricity to power 105,000 houses. The ship's freezers make 110,230 pounds of ice cubes a day—more than the weight of nine adult elephants. A crew of thirty-four, mostly from Indonesia, launders more than 20,000 towels, sheets, and tablecloths per day. And the priciest suite goes for $34,000 a week. **What you can do:** If you want to experience *Oasis of the Seas,* expect to pay between about $1,500 and $3,500 for a week's cruise.

HOW LONG DOES IT TAKE TO RACE UP THE STAIRS TO THE OBSERVATION DECK OF THE EMPIRE STATE BUILDING?
About 325 people sign up for the annual race—the Empire State Building Run-up—and the winner usually can do it in slightly more than ten minutes. For the record, it's eighty-six floors and 1,576 steps to the observation deck, but the racers go two steps at a time, so they touch only 788 steps.

WHEN IT COMES TO HOUSING, NEW YORK CITY IS KNOWN FOR ITS HIGH-RISE CONDOS, BROWN-STONES AND TENEMENT APARTMENT BUILDINGS, BUT FEW PEOPLE, EVEN LONGTIME RESIDENTS, REALIZE THE CITY OFFERS ANOTHER HOUSING OPTION. WHAT IS IT?
Trailer parks. Actually, there's only one. It's on Staten Island, and it's called Goethals Community, where 128 single-wides sit on a lot next to a marsh, another unfamiliar site in New York City. Residents pay $500 a month to rent narrow lots for their fourteen- by seventy-foot homes. The trailer park only exists because in 1969 its developers found a loophole in a city law that allowed trailer parks on land zoned for manufacturing. The loophole has since been closed, ensuring that the city will have no other trailer parks.

F. SCOTT FITZGERALD IS KNOWN AS MUCH FOR HIS ROLLICKING, EXCESSIVE, HIGHBROW LIFE-STYLE THAT CHARACTERIZED THE ROARING TWENTIES AS FOR HIS NOVELS, INCLUDING *THE GREAT GATSBY, THE BEAUTIFUL AND DAMNED, THIS SIDE OF PARADISE* AND *TENDER IS THE NIGHT.* IN 1936, HOW MUCH DID HE RECEIVE IN BOOK ROYALTIES?
Eighty dollars. Fitzgerald, who received as much as $4,000 for a short story as late as 1930—the equivalent of $51,000 today—went through hard times starting in the early

1930s due to his abuse of alcohol and drugs, his writing difficulties, and the mental breakdown and hospitalization of his wife, who required much of his time and attention. All of this led to his fall from grace with readers. For example, *Tender Is the Night*, which was published in 1934, was not critically acclaimed at the time and did not sell well during his lifetime. Fitzgerald died in Hollywood in 1940, at the age of forty-four.

CURIOUS GEORGE, THE MISCHIEVOUS AND LOVABLE MONKEY, ESCAPED AN ELEVATOR OPERATOR, FARMER, COOK, ZOOKEEPERS AND FIREFIGHTERS, ALL OF WHOM WANTED A PIECE OF HIM FOR VARIOUS REASONS. BUT HOW DID HIS CREATORS, MARGRET AND H. A. REY, TOP HIS FREQUENT ESCAPES?

The Reys, who were Jewish, fled France on two pieced-together bicycles two days before the Nazis invaded Paris in 1940. They traveled seventy-five miles in their first three days on the road, the start of a four-month journey that led them to Lisbon, Rio de Janeiro, and finally New York. **Bonus question: Why was Curious George called Zozo in Great Britain?** The book's British publisher didn't think King George VI, the reigning monarch at the time, would appreciate sharing a name with a literary monkey, especially because "curious" more accurately equates to "strange" in Britain.

HOW OFTEN DO WE BLINK PER MINUTE?

That depends on how we're feeling, what we're doing, and how old we are. A nervous adult blinks fifty times per minute while a calm adult blinks fifteen times per minute. When we're staring at the TV, we blink only seven and a half times per minute. Newborns blink only twice per minute, perhaps because they're so busy taking in their new surroundings and because tired eyes blink more, and infants tend to sleep when they're tired while adults sometimes aren't able to do that. **What you can do:** If your eyes blink rapidly or rarely, see a doctor. Blinking eyes can help doctors diagnose medical conditions. For example, rapid blinking may signal the onset of Tourette's syndrome, strokes, or nervous system problems. A person who rarely blinks may have Parkinson's disease.

IF SOMEONE HITS YOU ON PURPOSE, DOES IT HURT MORE THAN IF IT WERE AN ACCIDENT?
Yes. A new study has confirmed earlier studies, which show this to be true. In the new study, more than forty volunteers were each given a partner. Some of the volunteers received electric shocks, none more severe than others. Of those who were shocked, some were told their partners administered the shocks while others were told they came from a computer. Those who were told the shocks came from their partners rated the shocks to be more painful than did those who were told the shocks were computer generated.

IF YOU LIVE IN THE UNITED STATES, AND YOU'RE DREAMING OF AN EXCEPTIONALLY WHITE CHRIST-MAS, WHERE DO YOU HAVE THE BEST CHANCE OF MAKING YOUR DREAM A REALITY?
Bettles, Alaska, population thirty-nine, in north central Alaska. There's a 100 percent chance that at least ten inches of snow will be on the ground on December 25, according to a recent government report. In the lower forty-eight, the snowiest place on Christ-mas Day is Stampede Pass, Washington, a mountain pass at 3,672 feet in the Cascade Mountains, where there is a 96 percent chance of seeing at least ten inches of snow on December 25. Other places where a white Christmas is very likely: most of Alaska, northern New England, and northern Michigan. The report's biggest surprises? Some places that are usually awfully cold on December 25 rarely see even a trace of snow on the ground that day. Here are the chances that you'll see any snow at all in these chilly places: Cincinnati (11 percent), New York City (10 percent), Philadelphia (10 percent), and Oklahoma City (3 percent). **Bonus question: In what year did Dallas experience its first Christmas Eve snowfall on record?** The first time was in 2009.

WHY IS IT SO HARD TO KEEP A NEW YEAR'S RESOLUTION?

Because our brains are overrated—or maybe overworked. That's right. Everyday events that tax our brains weaken our discipline, whether we're trying to avoid a cigarette, a beer, or a cupcake. In one experiment involving Stanford University undergrads, one group was given a two-digit number to remember and another, a seven-digit number. Shortly afterward, the students were offered fruit salad or chocolate cake. Those who were asked to memorize a seven-digit number were nearly twice as likely to choose the cake. Researchers say those students' brains experienced a "cognitive load," which reduced their ability to resist temptation and led them to make an unhealthy choice. **What you can do:** Want to keep your New Year's resolution? First of all, make just one resolution, not two, three, or four. Then incorporate it into your life: If you resolve to work out three times a week, schedule three workouts a week as if they are meetings with an important client. Don't be afraid to seek help to keep your resolution, especially if it will make you healthier. If you want to work out three times a week, find a workout partner or someone else who will hold you accountable.

CHILDREN OF OLDER FATHERS ARE BETTER OFF BECAUSE THEIR DADS ARE WISER, WEALTHIER AND MORE MATURE, RIGHT?

Apparently not. A study that followed 33,437 children found that young children of dads in their mid to late forties scored lower on IQ and other tests, regardless of the mothers' ages. Other studies found that teenagers with older dads scored lower on non-verbal tests and were more likely to suffer from schizophrenia and autism. Researchers speculate that something changes in sperm over time—perhaps gene mutations—to contribute to these disadvantages.

IS YOUR CHILD BETTER OFF WITH A VERY GOOD TEACHER IN A BAD SCHOOL OR WITH A BAD TEACHER IN A VERY GOOD SCHOOL?

The former. Researchers say students with bad teachers learn half of what they should in a school year while students with very good teachers learn a year and a half's worth of material.

WHAT PERCENTAGE OF AN AMERICAN CHILD'S LIFE IS SPENT UNDER A SCHOOL ROOF?
Nine. And that assumes the child attended full-day kindergarten and had perfect attendance throughout elementary, middle, and high school. This fact is a sore subject for a growing number of American educators and others who regret that other nations' children who spend more time in school perform better on global standardized tests. Chinese students, for example, are in school forty-one more days per school year than are Americans. **Bonus question: How much time do kindergarteners in the nation's two largest school districts, New York and Los Angeles, spend on test preparation and on unstructured playtime?** An average of twenty-four minutes a day on test preparation and twenty-five minutes a day on unstructured playtime.

WHEN IS THE BEST TIME FOR RECESS—BEFORE OR AFTER LUNCH?
Before. Students who go out for recess before lunch eat more of their lunch, go to the nurse's office less often, and behave better in the afternoon, according to recent studies. By the time these students get to the cafeteria, they're hungrier, and they waste less food. Some schools that schedule recess before lunch report that students eat more fruits and vegetables and drink more milk and water than students at schools who have recess after lunch. And fewer students complain of stomachaches because they're not running around the playground on a full stomach. **The downside to a morning recess?** Some kids are dirty when they arrive in the cafeteria for lunch. Although the pros seem to outweigh the cons, many schools just don't like change. Only about 5 percent of schools schedule recess before lunch. **Bonus question: If a student misbehaves, is it a good idea to punish him by making**

him stay indoors during recess? No. As a part of a larger study involving about 11,000 third graders, researchers found that students who received at least fifteen minutes of recess a day tended to behave better in class. This information helps educators make a compelling argument, the researchers say, that schools need to be designed and built with plenty of outdoor places for children to run and play.

HOW MANY ALLEGEDLY INCOMPETENT AND ABUSIVE NEW YORK CITY PUBLIC SCHOOL TEACHERS ARE PAID TO DO NOTHING?

About 625. These teachers, who are represented by the United Federation of Teachers, are sent to one of seven "temporary reassignment centers"—sarcastically referred to as rubber rooms—where they must show up Mondays through Fridays while their cases make their way through the school district's bureaucratic alleys—sometimes as long as three years. The teachers, who may sleep, read, or do whatever they wish in the rubber rooms, earn their pay as well as pension benefits. Some earn six-figure salaries.

ONLY ABOUT HALF OF ALL COLLEGE ENTRANTS GRADUATE WITHIN SIX YEARS, BUT THAT GROUP MUST BE WELL PREPARED TO MAKE IT IN THE REAL WORLD, RIGHT?

Not exactly. One study concluded that only 38 percent of college graduates, when asked to read two newspaper editorials with differing views, could accurately compare the views. **Bonus question: In 2006 what percentage of twelfth graders could explain why the United States became involved in the Korean War?** Fourteen.

DO OTHERS REALLY LOOK BETTER AS WE DRINK MORE ALCOHOL?

Yes, if they're older and wearing a lot of makeup, say researchers who interviewed 240 people. But the drinkers didn't feel this way about underage girls. Even those who drank a lot of alcohol didn't think the girls were older and prettier than they were. The research hurts the cases of adults—mostly men—who have used alcohol as an excuse to have sex with minors. **What you can do:** Drink a glass of water after every bottle of beer or glass of wine you consume. Water dulls the effect of the alcohol.

WHEN IT COMES TO DETECTING UNDERARM ODOR, WHO'S BETTER—MEN OR WOMEN?

Women. And it's not even close, according to a study of twenty men and twenty women. The researchers used other fragrances to try to mask underarm odor, but the women detected it almost every time. The researchers speculate that women may use this skill to help influence how they choose their mates. **What you can do:** Other than bathing daily and using deodorant, there are a lot of things you can try if your body odor is especially bad: (1) place a teaspoon of hydrogen peroxide in a glass of water, stir, and use the mixture to wash under your arms; (2) wear loose-fitting clothing that allows sweat to escape; (3) avoid tobacco, meat, onions, garlic, spices, coffee, and alcohol, which can exacerbate body odor; (4) take supplements, such as chlorophyll, magnesium, B vitamins, and zinc, which sometimes help reduce body odor; and (5) get a complete physical exam. Kidney or liver disease also can cause body odor.

HOW MANY WOMEN ARE HEAD COACHES OF HIGH SCHOOL VARSITY FOOTBALL TEAMS IN THE UNITED STATES?

One. Natalie Randolph, a former track athlete at the University of Virginia who played six seasons for the D.C. Divas of the National Women's Football Association, became head coach of Calvin Coolidge Senior High School in Washington, DC, in 2010. **Bonus question: The Mohegans, an American Indian tribe, did something in 2010 that it hadn't done since 1723. What was that?** It elected a woman to be its chief. In August 2010 Lynn Malerba became chief of one of the most prosperous American Indian tribes in the nation. The Mohegans operate the Mohegan Sun casino complex, which employs nearly 10,000 people in southeastern Connecticut. The position of chief had been vacant since October 2007, when the former chief died.

WHICH BOOK OF THE BIBLE MAKES NO MENTION OF GOD AND AVOIDS ANY REFERENCE TO PRAYING AND WORSHIPPING?

Esther, in the Old Testament. The author, who is unknown, wrote about a festival and the deliverance of the Jews during the reign of Xerxes. The fact that God is not mentioned has triggered debate about the book's religious value, but some argue that the author assumes God controls everything, so there is no reason to mention him. **Bonus question: Most people know the Bible sells better than even Harry Potter, and many people know Psalms, with its 150 chapters, is the longest book of the Bible, but which book in the Bible contains the largest number of different words?** Isaiah. The prophet Isaiah had quite a vocabulary and used nearly 2,200 different words. By the way, some scholars question whether he wrote all sixty-six chapters, but there are similarities throughout the book that make a good case for his solo authorship.

HOW MANY HOTELS DOES THE MASSIVE RITZ-CARLTON HOTEL COMPANY OWN?

Zero. With its 38,000 or so employees, the company *manages* the seventy-five Ritz-Carlton hotels but owns none of them. Marriott International does. Eight additional Ritz-Carlton hotels are scheduled to open starting in 2011.

WHY DO CONSTRUCTION-RELATED ACCIDENTS IN NEW YORK CITY OFTEN OCCUR ON FRIDAYS?

Because workers start drinking alcohol to jumpstart their weekend plans, according to the city's Department of Investigation, which looks into fraud and corruption among city employees and those who work with them. That's consistent with what economists and others say about productivity on Fridays. Workers tend to need more supervision and be less productive on that day because their minds wander as they begin thinking about the coming weekend. **What you can do:** If you run a company, Friday is the best day of the week to shut things down for a company-wide meeting. The worst day? Tuesday, widely considered the most productive day of the week.

THOUSANDS OF PRODUCTS—SOME SAY MORE THAN 5,000—COME FROM TREES AND THEIR BY-PRODUCTS. WHAT ARE SOME OF THE MORE UNUSUAL ONES?

Crayons, deodorant, ice cream, adhesives, paints, ink, chewing gum, fireworks, medicine, shoe polish, film, glass, imitation sponges, imitation leather, dyes, flavorings, charcoal, tar, oil, tea, and sports drinks. Torula yeast, a high-protein product that comes from wood sugars, is an ingredient in baby foods, cereals, imitation bacon, pet foods, and baked goods.

SOURCES

Most of the answers to the questions you just read didn't include attribution, but the information came from reliable sources, which are listed here:

1

Why are hospitals so worried about neckties?—Rebecca Smith, reporter, "Nothing to Sneeze At: Doctors' Neckties Seen as Flu Peril," *Wall Street Journal*, November 19, 2009.

How many different species of bacteria are on your hands right now, and why are law enforcement officials excited to know that?—Noah Fierer, assistant professor, University of Colorado, et al., "Forensic Identification Using Skin Bacterial Communities," *Proceedings of the National Academy of Sciences*, March 16, 2010; Anahad O'Connor, columnist, "REALLY? The Claim: Always Wash Your Hands With Hot Water, Not Cold," *New*

York Times, October 12, 2009; Ramanakumar V. Agnihotram, postdoctoral fellow, University of Montreal, "An Overview of Occupational Health Research in India," *Indian Journal of Occupational and Environmental Medicine*, April 2005.

If you're trying to choose just the right doctor, what's one of the most important things you need to find out?—Filip Lievens, professor of psychology, Ghent University, Belgium, et al., "Personality Scale Validities Increase Throughout Medical School," *Journal of Applied Psychology*, November 2009; Anemona Hartocollis, metro reporter, "Getting Into Med School Without Hard Sciences," *New York Times*, July 29, 2010.

Bad bosses can be a pain in the you-know-what. Where else can they be a pain?—Anna Nyberg, lead researcher, Department of Public Health Sciences, Karolinska Institute, et al., "Managerial Leadership and Ischaemic Heart Disease Among Employees: The Swedish WOLF Study," *Occupational and Environmental Medicine*, November 25, 2008; Dennis Nishi, contributing writer, "What to Do If Your Boss Is the Problem," *Wall Street Journal*, April 20, 2010.

Counting sheep is so boring that it's bound to put you to sleep, but does it really work?—Allison Harvey, associate professor of psychology, Oxford University, et al., "The Management of Unwanted Pre-Sleep Thoughts in Insomnia: Distraction With Imagery Versus General Distraction," *Behaviour Research and Therapy*, March 2002.

Why is it so important to be fit in your fifties?—Ron Winslow, deputy bureau chief, health and science, "To Double the Odds of Seeing 85: Get a Move On," *Wall Street Journal*, March 9, 2010; I. Min Lee, associate professor, Harvard Medical School and Brigham and Women's Hospital, et al., "Physical Activity and Weight Gain Prevention," *Journal of the American Medical Association*, March 24/31, 2010.

If you're in your early sixties, what are the odds that you'll need nursing home care at some point during your life?—"The 2009 MetLife Market Survey of Nursing Homes, Assisted Living, Adult Day Services and Home Care Costs," MetLife Mature Market Institute, October 2009.

How much hair do we lose every day?—Lesley Alderman, Patient Money columnist, "When Hair Loss Strikes, a Doctor Is a Girl's Best Friend," *New York Times*, January 15, 2010.

There's a global shortage of kidneys for transplants, and only one country has no shortage. Which is it?—Alex Tabarrok, professor of economics, George Mason University, "The Meat Market," *Wall Street Journal*, January 9–10, 2010; World Health Organization; Dorry L. Segev, associate professor of surgery, Johns Hopkins University, et al., "Perioperative Mortality and Long-term Survival Following Live Kidney Donation," *Journal of the American Medical Association*, March 10, 2010; Organ Procurement and Transplantation Network.

Just about all of us have had our hearts broken, but can a heart really break?—Ron Winslow, deputy bureau chief, health and science, "Hearts Actually Can Break," *Wall Street Journal*, February 9, 2010.

By now most of us know that eating a lot of fish helps your heart stay healthy, but is there any other good reason to eat it?—Emiliano Albanese, clinical epidemiologist at King's College London, et al., "Dietary Fish and Meat Intake and Dementia in Latin America, China, and India: A 10/66 Dementia Research Group Population-based Study," *American Journal of Clinical Nutrition*, August 2009.

Atherosclerosis, or hardening of the arteries, is widely believed to be a modern disease, the product of too much fast food and too little exercise. True?—Adel H. Allam, doctor, Al Azhar Medical School, Cairo, et al., "Computed Tomographic Assessment of Atherosclerosis in Ancient Egyptian Mummies," *Journal of the American Medical Association*, November 18, 2009.

Marijuana has been proven to help relieve pain and curb nausea, and in recent years an increasing number of states have legalized it. But how addictive is it compared with other drugs?—Anna Wilde Mathews, health columnist, "Is Marijuana a Medicine?" *Wall Street Journal*, January 19, 2010.

Would it be such a big deal if we didn't have our pinkie fingers?—Dana Scarton, journalist, "Get Along Without a Pinkie? It's Tougher Than You Might Think," *New York Times*, December 16, 2008.

What about your toes? If you can't touch them, does that mean you're an out-of-shape slob who's going to die before your time?—Kenta Yamamoto, researcher, University of North Texas, et al., "Poor Trunk Flexibility Is Associated With Arterial Stiffening," *Heart and Circulatory Physiology*, October 2009.

Multivitamins have a little of everything that our bodies need, but can they be counted on to help prevent serious disease, as so many people believe?—Marian L. Neuhouser, nutritional epidemiologist, Fred Hutchinson Cancer Research Center, Seattle, et al., "Multivitamin Use and Risk of Cancer and Cardiovascular Disease in the Women's Health Initiative Cohorts," *Archives of Internal Medicine*, February 9, 2009; Anna Wilde Mathews, health columnist, "The Danger of Daily Aspirin," *Wall Street Journal*, February 23, 2010.

Can blind people see anything when they dream?—Anahad O'Connor, reporter, "The Claim: Blind People Do Not See Images in Their Dreams," *New York Times*, December 16, 2008.

How many times a day do Americans show up in a hospital emergency room because their cat or dog caused them to fall?—"Nonfatal Fall-Related Injuries Associated with Dogs and Cats—United States, 2001–2006," *Morbidity and Mortality Weekly Report*, March 27, 2009.

The 2010 earthquake in Haiti that killed more than 200,000 people inflicted additional pain on injured Haitians for months afterward. Why?—Ianthe Jeanne Dugan, senior staff writer, "Emergency Doctors Leave Haiti," *Wall Street Journal*, February 24, 2010; Andrew C. Revkin, reporter, "Disaster Awaits Cities in Earthquake Zones," *New York Times*, February 24, 2010.

What percentage of Americans over sixty-five have no natural teeth?—Centers for Disease Control and Prevention; National Institute of Dental and Craniofacial Research; American Academy of Periodontology.

Is there a connection between the occurrence of headaches and the weather?—Kenneth J. Mukamal, doctor, Beth Israel Deaconess Medical Center, Boston, et al., "Weather and Air Pollution as Triggers of Severe Headaches," *Neurology*, March 10, 2009.

What's the best remedy for chronic headaches?—Yanxia Sun, research associate, Tong J. Gan, professor and vice-chair, Department of Anesthesia, Duke University Medical Center, "Acupuncture for the Management of Chronic Headache: A Systematic Review," *Anesthesia and Analgesia*, December 2008.

If you're an adult trying to dodge the flu, what makes more sense—getting a shot of the vaccine or getting the nasal spray?—Zhong Wang, researcher, Armed Forces Health Surveillance Center, Silver Spring, Md., et al., "Live Attenuated or Inactivated Influenza Vaccines and Medical Encounters for Respiratory Illnesses Among US Military Personnel," *Journal of the American Medical Association*, March 2, 2009.

As many as one-third of children in public housing suffer from asthma. Why?—Elissa Ely, doctor and contributing writer, "House Dust Yields Clue to Asthma: Roaches," *New York Times*, April 7, 2009.

Who's better able to function well without sleep: the old or the young?—Jeanne F. Duffy, Hannah J. Willson, Wei Wang, and Charles A. Czeisler, researchers, Brigham and Women's Hospital, Boston, "Healthy Older Adults Better Tolerate Sleep Deprivation Than Young Adults," *Journal of the American Geriatrics Society*, May 3, 2009.

It's common knowledge that poor health leads to unemployment, but does unemployment lead to poor heath?—Roni Caryn Rabin, freelance writer, "Losing Job May Be Hazardous to Health," *New York Times*, May 9, 2009.

It has been noted that U.S. presidents who enter office with brown or black hair leave with gray. Is this because that job is the most stressful on the planet?—J. M. Wood, professor, Queensland University of Technology, Brisbane, Australia, et al., "Senile Hair Graying: H_2O_2-mediated Oxidative Stress Affects Human Hair Color by Blunting Methionine Sulfoxide Repair," *FASEB (Federation of American Societies for Experimental Biology) Journal*, February 2009; Alison Johnson, contributing writer, "How to . . . Guard Against Gray Hair," *Daily Press*, January 9, 2010.

When it comes to weight, which country is most likely to ignore doctors' advice, and which is most likely to use smoking as a weight-loss strategy?—Joe Kita, writer, "Global Poll: A Look at Weight Around the World," *Reader's Digest*, February 2010.

Which country feels the most pressure to lose weight, and which country is most likely to do something about it?—Joe Kita, writer, "Global Poll: A Look at Weight Around the World," *Reader's Digest*, February 2010.

Are overweight children less likely to be injured in a car crash because they have more padding?—Keshia M. Pollack, assistant professor, Johns Hopkins Bloomberg School of Public Health, et al., "Body Mass Index and Injury Risk Among U.S. Children 9–15 Years Old in Motor Vehicle Crashes," *Injury Prevention*, December 2008; National Health and Nutrition Examination Survey.

Are you more likely to be fat if you live near a fast-food restaurant?—National Bureau of Economic Research, National Restaurant Association.

Do food ads on TV simply promote competition between companies selling similar brands, as the industry has long claimed, or do the ads cause the people watching them to eat more?—Alex Mindlin, freelance writer, "Snack Ads Spur Children to Eat More," *New York Times*, July 20, 2009; Sandeep Ravindran, editorial intern, "Sweet Sensor," *Popular Science*, March 2010.

If I'm sleeping less, am I eating more?—National Sleep Foundation; Centers for Disease

Control and Prevention; Jill Waldbieser, freelance journalist, "We're Losing Sleep and Gaining Weight," *Popular Science*, March 2009.

Which is the most obese country in the world?—Global Database on Body Mass Index, World Health Organization; Centers for Disease Control and Prevention.

OK, Americans are fat, but how fat?—Elizabeth Kolbert, staff writer, "XXXL: Why are we so fat?" *New Yorker*, July 20, 2009; School Nutrition Association; Eric Finkelstein and Laurie Zuckerman, *The Fattening of America* (Wiley, 2009); Roni Caryn Rabin, freelance writer, "Obese Americans Spend Far More on Health Care," *New York Times*, July 28, 2009.

If you're about ten to fifteen pounds overweight, how much are you hurting yourself?—Katherine Rosman, reporter, "A Case for Those Extra 10 Pounds," *Wall Street Journal*, April 27, 2010; Shirley S. Wang, reporter, "A New Way to Lose Weight?" *Wall Street Journal*, April 13, 2010.

What's more dangerous to your health: smoking or obesity?—Martin Neovius, postdoctoral fellow, Karolinska Institute, Stockholm, et al., "Combined Effects of Overweight and Smoking in Late Adolescence on Subsequent Mortality: Nationwide Cohort Study," *British Medical Journal*, March 2009; Centers for Disease Control and Prevention.

Most people know smoking can lead to heart disease. In fact, a smoker is six times more likely to suffer from heart problems, making it the top predictor for heart disease. Which is the second-highest predictor?—G. David Batty, Wellcome Trust fellow and scientist, Medical Research Council, in Glasgow, Scotland, et al., "Does IQ Predict Cardiovascular Disease Mortality as Strongly as Established Risk Factors? Comparison of Effect Estimates Using the West of Scotland Twenty-07 Cohort Study," *European Journal of Cardiovascular Prevention & Rehabilitation*, February 2010; Vasudev Ananthram, cardiologist, "Getting to the Heart of the Matter," *Health Journal*, February 2010.

You've heard it a million times: Smoking cigarettes causes cancer, heart disease, and stroke, just to name three. Can there possibly be a downside to quitting?—Hsin-Chieh Yeh, assistant professor of internal medicine, Johns Hopkins University School of Medicine, et al., "Smoking, Smoking Cessation, and Risk for Type 2 Diabetes Mellitus: A Cohort Study," *Annals of Internal Medicine*, January 5, 2010; Honglei Chen, doctor, National Institute of Environmental Health Sciences, "Smoking Duration, Intensity, and Risk of Parkinson Disease," *Neurology*, March 10, 2010.

How many people smoke in the United States, and what's the trend?—Centers for Disease Control and Prevention; Melinda Beck, health reporter and columnist, "Rise of the Part-Time Smoker," *Wall Street Journal*, January 12, 2010.

If you have friends or loved ones who smoke and you really want them to stop, will it help to pay them?—Kevin G. Volpp, associate professor of medicine and health care management, University of Pennsylvania School of Medicine, et al., "A Randomized, Controlled Trial of Financial Incentives for Smoking Cessation," *New England Journal of Medicine*, February 12, 2009.

If there's one city in America that believes all of the studies about the dangers of secondhand smoke, which is it?—R. N. Alsever, doctor, Parkview Medical Center, Colorado, "Reduced Hospitalizations for Acute Myocardial Infarction After Implementation of a Smoke-Free Ordinance," Centers for Disease Control and Prevention's *Morbidity and Mortality Weekly Report*, January 2, 2009.

What percentage of doctors in China smoke?—Nick Macfie, reporter, "China Urges Smoking Doctors to Quit the Habit," Reuters, March 2, 2009; Centers for Disease Control and Prevention; ChinaToday.com; China Consumers Association; Melinda Beck, health reporter and columnist, "Checking Up on the Doctor," *Wall Street Journal*, May 25, 2010.

Something else everyone knows: Walking is great exercise, but how fast do you have to walk to reap

the best benefits?—Simon J. Marshall, professor, School of Exercise and Nutritional Sciences at San Diego State University, et al., "Translating Physical Activity Recommendations into a Pedometer-Based Step Goal: 3000 Steps in 30 Minutes," *American Journal of Preventive Medicine*, May 2009.

China has invested untold billions in green energy technology during the past twenty years, but in 2006 it passed the United States as the world's largest producer of greenhouse gases. Just how bad is it in Beijing?—Evan Osnos, writer, "Green Giant: Beijing's Crash Program for Clean Energy," *New Yorker*, December 21, 28, 2009.

Americans are more educated about the importance of exercising, smoking, and eating fruits and vegetables, so what have they done with that knowledge?—National Center for Health Statistics' surveys, 1988–94 and 2001–06.

So, *you* manage to eat healthy and feed your children plenty of fruits and vegetables. That means they'll grow up and follow your example, right?—May A. Beydoun, postdoctoral fellow, and Youfa Wang, assistant professor, Johns Hopkins School of Public Health, "Parent-Child Dietary Intake Resemblance in the United States: Evidence from a Large Representative Survey," *Social Science and Medicine*, June 2009.

Which countries by percentage have the most undernourished people?—2008 World Population Data Sheet; multiple authors, "Tracking Progress on Child and Maternal Nutrition," Unicef, November 2009; Harper's Index, *Harper's*, February 2010.

In 1971, President Richard Nixon said we should cure cancer by 1976. How are we doing on that goal?—National Center for Health Statistics; National Cancer Institute.

Do cancer patients in support groups live longer than those who don't receive support?—David Spiegel, professor, psychiatry and behavioral science at Stanford University, et al., "Effects of Supportive-Expressive Group Therapy on Survival of Patients with Metastatic Breast Cancer: A Randomized Prospective Trial," *Cancer*, September 2007; Abby Ellin, reporter, "Seeking a Cure for Optimism," *New York Times*, December 30, 2009.

If you suffered a stroke, would you know it?—Christiane Reitz, postdoctoral research scientist, Columbia University Medical Center, et al., "Validity of Self-Reported Stroke in Elderly African Americans, Caribbean Hispanics, and Whites," *Archives of Neurology*, May 11, 2009.

Who naps more: the employed or the unemployed?—Paul Taylor, researcher, Pew Research Center, "Nap Time," PewResearch.org, July 29, 2009.

Oxytocin, a hormone produced by the pituitary gland, is best known for regulating bodily functions, such as a woman's ability to deliver milk to her child, and for fostering bonds between mother and child. Is there more to it than that?—Ernst Fehr, director of the Institute for Empirical Research in Economics at the University of Zurich, et al., "Oxytocin Increases Trust in Humans," *Nature*, June 2, 2005.

What can you buy for two cents these days?—John Conroy, writer, "The Virtue of Small Change: Rescuing the World Costs Less Than You Think," *Rotarian*, November 2009.

How about three cents?—Nicholas D. Kristof, foreign affairs columnist, "Attack of the Worms," *New York Times*, July 2, 2007; Annemarie Mannion, freelance writer, "Sweat the Small Stuff," *Rotarian*, February 2010; Global Network for Neglected Tropical Diseases.

2

Of the 446 men and women who have been executed in Texas since 1976, when the Supreme Court reinstated the death penalty, what was the most used word spoken during their last-words speeches?—Ian Yarrett, reporter, "What's the Last Word in Capital Punishment?" *Newsweek*, November 30, 2009.

Killer cows?—W. T. Sanderson and M. D. Madsen, researchers, Great Plains Center for Agricultural Health and the Injury Prevention Research Center, University of Iowa,

"Fatalities Caused by Cattle—Four States, 2003–2008," *Morbidity and Mortality Weekly Report*, Centers for Disease Control and Prevention, July 31, 2009.

Which is the most dangerous day of the year to drive a car?—Charles M. Farmer, director of statistical services, and Allan F. Williams, senior vice-president for research, Insurance Institute for Highway Safety, "Temporal Factors in Motor Vehicle Crash Deaths," *Injury Prevention*, 2005; Insurance Institute for Highway Safety's Highway Loss Data Institute.

How about for pedestrians?—Charles M. Farmer, director of statistical services, and Allan F. Williams, senior vice-president for research, Insurance Institute for Highway Safety, "Temporal Factors in Motor Vehicle Crash Deaths," *Injury Prevention*, 2005; Insurance Institute for Highway Safety's Highway Loss Data Institute.

What percentage of students said choking yourself in an attempt to get high poses no risk?—Sarah K. Ramowski, adolescent health policy specialist, Oregon Public Health Division, et al., " 'Choking Game' Awareness and Participation Among 8th Graders—Oregon, 2008," *Morbidity and Mortality Weekly Report*, Centers for Disease Control and Prevention, January 15, 2010; Andrew J. Macnab, professor, Department of Pediatrics, University of British Columbia, et al., "Asphyxial Games or 'The Choking Game': A Potentially Fatal Risk Behaviour," *Injury Prevention*, 2009.

Humans can tolerate an awful lot of abuse, but what are our live-or-die limits?—Shelley Sperry, senior researcher, "Human Limits," *National Geographic*, October 2009.

In a recent survey of 1,007 American adults, 82 percent said they would survive just fine without power for two weeks during a winter storm that made it impossible to leave home. What percentage had all of the necessary items to live comfortably?—"Stock Your Emergency Kit," *Consumer Reports*, January 2010.

What are the odds of dying in a car crash versus on a roller coaster?—Stuart Fox, writer, "Statistically Speaking," *Popular Science*, November 2008.

If you're on an airplane that fails in midair, what are the chances that you'll survive?—Dan Koeppel, contributing writer, "Taking a Fall," *Popular Mechanics*, February 2010; Nicola Clark, staff writer, "Jet Crashes in Libya; Boy Is Said to Be Sole Survivor," *New York Times*, May 12, 2010.

What color is an airplane's flight data recorder, or "black box"?—Jack Curry, contributing writer, "Why Plane Crashes Happen," *Parade*, July 19, 2009; Denis and Chloé Beaudouin, *Charles Beaudouin: Une Histoire D'instruments Scientifiques* (EDP Sciences Editions, 2005).

How many people die every year because a doctor, nurse, or other caregiver makes a mistake, and what are hospitals doing about it?—Laura Landro, assistant managing editor/health columnist, "New Focus on Averting Errors: Hospital Culture," *Wall Street Journal*, March 16, 2010.

How many serial killers and serial killings are there in the United States every year?—U.S. Justice Department; Jessica Snyder Sachs, contributing editor, "Anatomy of a Serial Killer," *Popular Science*, January 2009; Joshua Buckholtz, graduate student, Vanderbilt University, et al., "Mesolimbic Dopamine Reward System Hypersensitivity in Individuals with Psychopathic Traits," *Nature Neuroscience*, March 14, 2010.

What percentage of all identifiable guns recovered from crime scenes in Mexico can be traced to U.S. gun shops?—U.S. Bureau of Alcohol, Tobacco and Firearms.

Which countries have the lowest and highest infant-mortality rates and where does the United States rank?—2008 World Population Data Sheet.

Which countries have the lowest and highest fertility rates?—2008 World Population Data Sheet.

How many children will die per year from 2009 to 2015 because of the global economic crisis, which began in 2008?—Shwetlena Sabarwal, Nistha Sinha, and Mayra Buvinic, economists, "The Global Financial Crisis: Assessing Vulnerability for Women and Children,"

Poverty Reduction and Economic Management Network of the World Bank, 2009.

Abortion rates have dropped sharply since 1990. Which states have the highest and lowest rates?—Rachel K. Jones, senior research associate, Guttmacher Institute, et al., "Abortion in the United States: Incidence of Access to Services, 2005," *Perspectives on Sexual and Reproductive Health*, March 2008.

In what year were the most babies born in the United States?—U.S. National Center for Health Statistics; American Medical Association.

Life expectancy in the United States continues to increase, but by how much?—U.S. Census Bureau; U.S. National Center for Health Statistics.

How much longer can we expect to live if the air we breathe is clean?—C. Arden Pope III, economics professor at Brigham Young University, et al., "Fine-Particulate Air Pollution and Life Expectancy in the United States," *New England Journal of Medicine*, January 29, 2009.

The vast majority of supercentenarians—people 110 and older—are women. Why?—Sarah Kliff, researcher, "Why Are All the Really Old People Women?" *Newsweek*, September 28, 2009; Census Bureau.

For years, psychologists have talked up how sunshine makes us happier, but is that always so?—Karin S. Björkstén, Daniel F. Kripke, and Peter Bjerregaard, researchers, "Accentuation of Suicides But Not Homicides with Rising Latitudes of Greenland in the Sunny Months," *BMC Psychiatry*, May 8, 2009.

Which country uses the death penalty more than any other?—"Death Sentences and Executions in 2008," Amnesty International, May 2009.

At least nine nations have nuclear weapons. Which are most likely to use them against each other, and what would happen to the environment if they did?—Alan Robock, professor of climatology, Rutgers University, and Owen Brian Toon, chair of the Department of Atmospheric and Oceanic Sciences, University of Colorado, Boulder, "Local Nuclear

War, Global Suffering," *Scientific American*, January 2010; Natural Resources Defense Council.

How many American lives are saved per month when gasoline costs $4 per gallon or more?—Michael Morrisey, professor of public health, University of Alabama at Birmingham, and Lee S. Friedman, Social Policy Research Institute, "Long-Term Effects of Repealing the National Maximum Speed Limit in the United States," *American Journal of Public Health*, July 16, 2009.

How can ice save your life?—Michael Holzer, cardiologist, "Mild Hypothermia to Improve the Neurologic Outcome After Cardiac Arrest," *New England Journal of Medicine*, February 21, 2002; Joerg C. Schefold and Christian Storm, cardiologists, Internal Intensive Care and Nephrology, Charité—Universitätsmedizin Berlin, "Mild Therapeutic Hypothermia After Cardiac Arrest and the Risk of Bleeding in Patients with Acute Myocardial Infarction," *International Journal of Cardiology*, March 6, 2009; American Heart Association.

How close can we get to the sun before we'd die?—Alessandra Calderin, editorial assistant, "FYI: Sometimes You Just Need to Know," *Popular Science*, August 2010.

3

If you had $10,000 to invest on October 1, 1964, what are some really smart things you should have done with it?—Sam Mamudi, reporter, "Buffett's Gains Beat Every Mutual Fund," *Wall Street Journal*, March 5, 2010.

Want to make money off hurricanes?—James Altucher, columnist, "Profiting From Disasters," *Wall Street Journal*, April 12, 2010.

How much does it cost to make a penny and a nickel?—Elizabeth Williamson, regulation and business lobbying reporter, "Will Nickel-Free Nickels Make a Dime's Worth of Difference?" *Wall Street Journal*, May 10, 2010.

What's the most anyone has paid for a penny?—Jeff D. Opdyke, reporter, "The Million-Dollar Penny," *Wall Street Journal*, November 19, 2009.

What's about the cheapest airfare you can get short of free?—AirAsia.

What's more: 3 dollars or 3 cents?—Ellen E. Furlong and John E. Opfer, economists, Ohio State University, "Cognitive Constraints on How Economic Rewards Affect Cooperation," *Psychological Science*, January 2009; Lindsay Pollock and Philip Boroff, reporters, "Warhol's '200 One Dollar Bills' Fetches $43.8 Million in N.Y.," *Bloomberg News*, November 12, 2009.

What will some folks do for $5?—Mary Pilon, reporter, "What Will People Do For Five Bucks?" *Wall Street Journal*, March 17, 2010.

If you bought a typewriter for $50 in 1963, what would it be worth in 2009?—Randy Kennedy, reporter, "Cormac McCarthy's Typewriter Brings $254,500 at Auction," *New York Times*, December 4, 2009; Sharon Tanenbaum, associate editor, "The Simple List," *Real Simple*, October 2010.

What percentage of American paper money contains traces of cocaine?—Yuegang Zuo, researcher, University of Massachusetts; American Chemical Society.

When it comes to cars, why is $25,000 considered a magic number?—Jonathan Welsh, reporter, "Why $25,000 Is Magic for Cars," *Wall Street Journal*, January 27, 2010.

Recessions are scary things, but do they have an upside?—Tamar Lewin, reporter, "A Hemline Index, Updated," *New York Times*, October 18, 2008; Timothy W. Martin, reporter, "Frugal Shoppers Drive Grocers Back to Basics," *Wall Street Journal*, June 24, 2009; Cory Nealon, reporter, "Trash is Down 28% from 2004," *Daily Press*, July 8, 2010.

Anything else good come out of recessions?—Abby Ellin, journalist, "The Recession. Isn't It Romantic?" *New York Times*, February 12, 2009; Smithsonian Institution; Weight Watchers; W. Bradford Wilcox, director of the National Marriage Project at the University of Virginia, "Can the Recession Save Marriage?" *Wall Street Journal*, December 11, 2009; Clare Ansberry, reporter, "Tinsel: Can't Live With It, Can't Get Past Christmas Without It," *Wall Street Journal*, December 23, 2009.

So, besides the obvious, what's the downside of a recession?—Andrew Adam Newman, contributing writer, "Pills Sales Rise as Financial Anxiety Chases the Sandman Away," *New York Times*, April 24, 2009.

The numbers of people who rely on food stamps also rise during recessions. Which places have the most people who receive food stamps? Which have the least?—Jason DeParle and Robert Gebeloff, reporters, "Food Stamp Use Soars and Stigma Fades," *New York Times*, November 28, 2009.

When times are tough, more people use coupons. Who's most likely to use them?—Timothy W. Martin, reporter, "Hard Times Turn Coupon Clipping Into the Newest Extreme Sport," *Wall Street Journal*, March 8, 2010.

Everyone knows Vegas casinos use overhead cameras to see what their guests are up to, but what else do they do to gather information?—Michael Kaplan, writer, "The Machines . . . Are Watching," *Popular Mechanics*, January 2010.

What's the most anyone has lost gambling in Las Vegas?—Alexandra Berzon, reporter, "The Gambler Who Blew $127 Million," *Wall Street Journal*, December 5–6, 2009.

What does it cost to station one U.S. soldier in Afghanistan?—Jesse Ellison, writer/reporter, "Million-Dollar Man," *Newsweek*, January 11, 2010.

It's an understatement to say that a lot of people want a piece of Bernard Madoff, who fleeced thousands of people out of billions of dollars in one of the largest Ponzi schemes in history. But how badly did they want a piece of Madoff's hunting gear?—Juliet Chung, reporter, "Madoff Auction Is Bounty for Victims," *Wall Street Journal*, November 16, 2009; Securities Investor Protection Corporation.

When it comes to shoplifting and employee theft, which country has the biggest problem?—Joshua Bamfield, director of the Centre for Retail Research, *Global Retail Theft Barometer*

2009, Centre for Retail Research, November 13, 2009.

A recent report of the largest retailers in forty-one countries found that 5.8 million people were apprehended for shoplifting in 2009. Were more of the thieves men or women?—Joshua Bamfield, director of the Centre for Retail Research, *Global Retail Theft Barometer 2009*, Centre for Retail Research, November 13, 2009.

How much does it cost to remove snow in New York City?—Brian K. Sullivan, reporter, "Washington Offices, NYC Schools Close as Storm Looms," *Bloomberg*, February 9, 2010; Peter N. Spencer, reporter, "City Calls on Residents to Help with Snow Removal," *Staten Island Advance*, December 19, 2009; Sudeep Reddy and Clare Ansberry, reporters, "States Face Big Costs to Dig Out from Blizzard," *Wall Street Journal*, February 9, 2010.

The bear market of 2007 to 2009 cost some investors as much as 60 percent of their investment portfolios before the markets began to rebound in March 2009. Despite this, what percentage of retirees in 2009 said they continued to invest in the stock market to try to achieve long-term gains?—BTN Research; Putnam Investments; *Brainy Quote*; Brett Arends, columnist, "The Oracle's Tips for the Rest of Us," *Wall Street Journal*, March 1, 2010.

When it comes to spending on health care and life expectancy, the citizens of which country get the most bang for their buck?—"OECD Health Data 2009," Organization for Economic Co-operation and Development, 2009.

How much does it cost to operate the average gasoline-powered car versus an electric car?—U.S. Department of Energy; Michael Belfore, contributing writer, "Charge 'Er Up," *Popular Mechanics*, December 2009.

What's the most anyone ever paid for a white truffle?—Laura Santini, reporter, "KKR's Deal Maker and Truffle Hunter," *Wall Street Journal*, November 19, 2009.

What's the most anyone ever paid for lunch?—David Barboza, business reporter, "Steak and Seafood, With a $14 Million Dessert," *New York Times*, July 4, 2009; Geoffrey

A. Fowler, reporter, "Lunch With the Oracle: $2.6 Million," *Wall Street Journal*, June 14, 2010.

How about a chair?—Kelly Crow, reporter, "Art Market Still in a Blue Period," *Wall Street Journal*, January 4, 2010.

A trio of investors in 2009 paid $1.2 million for a three-year-old cow from Canada named Missy. Why in the world would anyone do that?—Erin Scottberg, research head, "$1.2 Million in Milk Money," *Popular Mechanics*, March 2010; "One Canadian Cow Sells for $1.2 Million," *United Press International*, November 12, 2009.

If money were no object, what's about the most you could pay for a new watch?—Richard Mille, watch manufacturer; Michael Clerizo, contributing editor, "Time Honored," *Wall Street Journal* magazine, May 2010.

How much will some people pay for a fish?—Yumiko Ono, staff reporter, "Tasting the $100,000 Tuna," *Wall Street Journal*, January 10–11, 2009; Yuka Hayashi, reporter, "The Land That Brought You Raw Fish Is Saying No to Seafood," *Wall Street Journal*, March 22, 2010.

How about the priciest hotel room in the world?—Sarah Nassauer, reporter, "A Room With a View, and a Price," *Wall Street Journal*, June 9, 2010.

You're a tree-hugger and you have more money than most of us. What can you do with your money around Christmastime?—Jennifer Steinhauer, reporter, "He Delivers Christmas Trees for Rent," *New York Times*, December 16, 2009; National Christmas Tree Association.

How much money do you have to make to increase your chances that the IRS will audit you?—"Earnings Under $200,000 Make an Audit Less Likely," *Associated Press*, December 23, 2009; Federal Reserve Survey of Consumer Finance.

How rare is it to be a billionaire in the United States?—Jeremy Berlin, editor, "Millionaires' Club," *National Geographic*, November 2008; *World Wealth Report 2008*, Capgemini/Merrill

Lynch; Spectrem Group, a wealth research firm; Carol J. Loomis, senior editor-at-large, "Fat Cat Pay—Then and Now," *Fortune*, November 18, 2009; Internal Revenue Service.

Speaking of millionaires, football coach Charlie Weis, who was called an offensive mastermind when he worked with professional athletes, bombed out after five seasons at Notre Dame, which paid him $36 million, including $18 million to leave before his contract ended. What could Notre Dame have bought for $36 million?—David Biderman, reporter, "What Else Could That Charlie Weis Money Buy?" *Wall Street Journal*, November 28–29, 2009.

As one of the world's largest exporters and importers, China certainly has embraced capitalism, no?—"Balance Sheet," *Newsweek*, July 20, 2009.

The mafia is into DVD piracy in a big way. Why?—Gregory F. Treverton, senior policy analyst, RAND Corporation, et al., *Film Piracy, Organized Crime and Terrorism* (RAND Corporation, 2009).

Tipping is more of an expected practice in U.S. restaurants than it is just about anywhere else in the world. How much tip money do American waiters and waitresses make per year?—Paul Wachter, freelance writer, "Why Tip?" *New York Times Magazine*, October 12, 2008.

If gasoline prices drop ten cents per gallon, how much money does that put in drivers' pockets nationwide?—Christopher Maag, freelance journalist, "Lower Gas Prices Don't Make Americans Feel Rich," *New York Times*, November 14, 2008; American Petroleum Institute.

Where is the most valuable vacant lot in the world?—Lingling Wei, Kris Hudson, and Christina S. N. Lewis, reporters, "Distress Calls Begin to Go Out," *Wall Street Journal*, January 6, 2010.

What's the most extreme example of rent-controlled apartments in the world?—Mike Esterl, reporter, "In This Picturesque Village, the Rent Hasn't Been Raised Since 1520," *Wall Street Journal*, December 26, 2008; Christine Haughney, reporter, "Vanishing Treasure: The Rent-Regulated Apartment," *New York Times*, May 24, 2010.

What is believed to be the biggest price cut for a single-family house in the United States?—Sara Lin, reporter, "A 52% Cut From $100 Million," *Wall Street Journal*, February 26, 2010; Christina S. N. Lewis, "Sign of the Times: Manor Price Cut by $50 Million," *Wall Street Journal*, April 21, 2009; Sara Lin and Juliet Chung, reporters, "Billionaire's Ex-Wife Asks $100 Million for Estate," *Wall Street Journal*, October 30, 2009; Census Bureau.

Which state saw the highest increases in home prices from the start of 2005 to the end of 2009, a period where the housing bubble burst and had yet to recover?—Federal Housing Finance Agency.

When will painting your walls bright pink cost you $3,500?—"The Eyes Have It: ODU Researchers Are First to Study Ocular Tracking in Subjects Viewing Real Estate Ads," Old Dominion University's Office of University Relations press release, July 29, 2010.

Who were the most unusual home buyers who took advantage of the $8,000 tax credit offered by the U.S. government in 2009 and 2010 to ease the nation's worst housing slump since the Great Depression?—Dawn Kopecki, reporter, "Four-Year-Olds Got Homebuyer Tax Credits, U.S. Says," *Bloomberg*, October 22, 2009; U.S. Department of the Treasury.

How many Americans work full-time year-round and still live below the poverty level?—U.S. Census Bureau, *Current Population Reports*, 2007.

What percentage of American families (by race) live below the poverty level?—U.S. Census Bureau, *Current Population Reports*, 2007.

What percentage of Americans say they live paycheck to paycheck? Of those, what percentage make more than $100,000 a year?—CareerBuilder.com; Employee Benefit Research Institute.

What percentage of retirees are still making monthly mortgage payments?—Society of Actuaries; Employee Benefit Research Institute; "A Happy Retirement: 6 Steps That Work," *Consumer Reports*, February 2010.

Of the nearly 7 billion people in the world today, about how many live on less than $1 a day?—World Bank; Joel K. Bourne Jr., contributing writer, "The End of Plenty," *National Geographic*, June 2009.

What percentage of children in the United States, the world's richest nation, live in poverty?—World Bank.

Who pays more for groceries: the rich or the poor?—Debabrata Talukdar, associate professor of marketing, State University of New York–Buffalo, "Cost of Being Poor: Retail Price and Consumer Price Search Differences across Inner-City and Suburban Neighborhoods," *Journal of Consumer Research*, July 2008.

You would be right to assume that the United States, the richest country in the world, has the most cars per 1,000 people. But which countries have the next most, and which have the least?—MotorIntelligence.com; China Association of Automobile Manufacturers; 2008 World Population Data Sheet.

Who tend to make more money: men who think women belong at home or men who think women belong wherever they want to be?—Timothy Judge, eminent scholar, and Beth Livingston, assistant professor, University of Florida, "Is the Gap More Than Gender? A Longitudinal Analysis of Gender, Gender Role Orientation, and Earnings," *Journal of Applied Psychology*, September 2008; U.S. Bureau of Labor Statistics.

If you're taller than the guy in the cubicle next to you, do you probably make more or less than him?—Anne Case, economist, Princeton University, et al., "Making Sense of the Labor Market from the British Household Panel Survey," National Bureau of Economic Survey working paper, May 2008.

Men make more money than women, but who has more purchasing power?—"Global Inquiry into Women and Consumerism," Boston Consulting Group, 2008.

How much does it cost to ship corn to Africa rather than just give seed and fertilizer to African

farmers?—Elizabeth Chiles Shelburne, freelance writer, "The Next Breadbasket?" *Atlantic*, September 2009.

How long does it take the cost of a public college education to catch up with the cost of a private college education?—College Board, U.S. Department of Labor.

Which college students make the most money in their first jobs?—National Association of Colleges and Employers; Mary Pilon, reporter, "What's a Degree Really Worth?" *Wall Street Journal*, February 2, 2010.

How much money do U.S. businesses lose during the first week of the NCAA basketball tournament because their employees sneak away to watch the games or follow them on their office computers?—Challenger, Gray & Christmas, an outplacement consulting firm; David Biderman, reporter, "There's No Place Like Home for Golden Lions," *Wall Street Journal*, January 12, 2009; Society for Human Resource Management.

4

Which beverage is more environmentally friendly: milk or beer?—Arjen Y. Hoekstra, professor, multidisciplinary water management, University of Twente, and scientific director, Water Footprint Network, Enschede, Netherlands. "The Water Footprint: Water in the Supply Chain," *The Environmentalist*, March 1, 2010.

Everyone says comparing apples and oranges is the wrong thing to do, but which one is more nutritious?—Marc Silver, deputy director of text, "Not Beyond Compare," *National Geographic*, March 2010.

How much more would a school lunch cost to remove the hot dogs, pizza, french fries, and other fast food from cafeterias and replace them with freshly prepared food?—Michael Pollan, writer, "Farmer in Chief," *New York Times Magazine*, October 12, 2008; Mary Kay Fox, senior researcher, et al., Mathematica Policy Research, Inc., Cambridge, Massachusetts, "Association Between School Food Environment and Practices and Body

Mass Index of U.S. Public School Children," *Journal of the American Dietetic Association*, February 2009; U.S. National Center for Education Statistics.

What are the eleven healthiest foods that are easy to find but only occasionally make their way into grocery carts?—Tara Parker-Pope, health reporter/columnist, "The 11 Best Foods You Aren't Eating," *New York Times*, June 30, 2008.

In which countries are you least and most likely to find vegetarians per capita?—Food and Agriculture Organization of the United Nations; Worldwatch Institute.

Americans love their burgers, bacon, and fried chicken. About how many animals have to give their lives each year to satisfy our appetites?—Jonathan Sarfan Foer, writer, *Eating Animals* (Little Brown, 2009).

Is McDonald's Filet-O-Fish sandwich really made with fish?—William J. Broad, reporter, "From Deep Pacific, Ugly and Tasty, With a Catch," *New York Times*, September 10, 2009.

Beachgoers tend to revile seaweed, but does it get a bum rap?—Patrick Barta, Asia correspondent, "Indonesia Got Soaked When the Seaweed Bubble Burst," *Wall Street Journal*, October 21, 2008.

What's the least healthy beverage you can drink?—Dave Zinczenko and Matt Goulding, writers, "The Unhealthiest Drinks in America 2009," *Men's Health*, July 7, 2009.

How much soda do Americans drink per year?—Mark Bittman, columnist, "Soda: A Sin We Sip Instead of Smoke?" *New York Times*, February 12, 2010; PepsiCo; Yale School of Medicine.

Once and for all, coffee: good or bad?—Melinda Beck, health reporter and columnist, "Good News in the Daily Grind," *Wall Street Journal*, December 29, 2009.

Plenty of studies these days trumpet the benefits of quaffing wine in moderation, but why are some doctors saying that's not always a good idea?—Roni Caryn Rabin, freelance writer, "Risks: Study Ties Alcohol to Recurrence of Breast Cancer," *New York Times*, December 10, 2009.

But if you don't have a history of breast cancer, there's nothing wrong with drinking one glass of wine per day, right?—Katri Räikkönen, researcher, University of Helsinki, "Prenatal Origins of Poor Sleep in Children," *Sleep*, August 1, 2009.

How seriously should you take the ratings you see on wine bottles?—Robert Hodgson, winemaker and statistician, "An Examination of Judge Reliability at a Major U.S. Wine Competition," *Journal of Wine Economics*, January 2009.

Everyone knows breast milk is the best thing you can give a newborn. If you're a baby born to a teenage mother, are you more likely to receive breast milk if your mother is white, black, or Mexican American?—U.S. National Center for Health Statistics.

How many poppy seed bagels could you make if Afghanistan set aside its entire annual crop for that innocent purpose?—Harper's Index, *Harper's*, July 2009; Food and Agriculture Organization Corporate Statistical Database.

Need another reason to like chocolate?—Maria Monagas, researcher at the University of Barcelona, et al., "Effect of Cocoa Powder on the Modulation of Inflammatory Biomarkers in Patients at High Risk of Cardiovascular Disease," *American Journal of Clinical Nutrition*, November 2009.

Need a reason to stay away from chocolate?—Natalie Rose, doctor, University of California at Davis, et al., "Chocolate and Depressive Symptoms in a Cross-Sectional Analysis," *Archives of Internal Medicine*, April 26, 2010.

Rice is arguably the most important food in the world, with global shortages translating to life-and-death situations for tens of millions of people. Is anything being done to ensure the world supply of it?—International Rice Research Institute.

The 2010 health care bill required restaurant chains to list the calories for food. How much do those menus influence what diners order?—New York City Department of Health and Mental Hygiene; Brian Elbel, assistant professor, Division of General Internal Medicine at New York University, "Calorie Labeling and Food Choices: A First Look at the Effects on Low-Income People In New York City," *Health Affairs*, October 6, 2009; Julie S. Downs, assistant research professor, George Loewenstein, professor, and Jessica Wisdom, graduate student, Department of Social and Decision Sciences, Carnegie Mellon University, "Strategies for Promoting Healthier Food Choices," *American Economic Review*, May 2009.

When it comes to figuring out how many calories are in food, Americans are pretty educated, right?— Scot Burton, professor of marketing, University of Arkansas, et al., "Attacking the Obesity Epidemic: The Potential Health Benefits of Providing Nutrition Information in Restaurants" *American Journal of Public Health*, September 2006.

How much swine waste does Smithfield Foods, the world's largest pork producer, flush into giant lagoons?—Jonathan Sarfan Foer, writer, *Eating Animals* (Little, Brown, 2009); U.S. Environmental Protection Agency; Smithfield Foods.

What does the apple-ring acacia tree in western Africa do that no other tree does, and why is that a good thing?—"Unique Acacia Tree's Promise To Revive African Soils," *ScienceDaily.com*, August 26, 2009; Katharine Gammon, freelance science writer, "The Giving Tree," *Popular Mechanics*, January 2010.

5

What are some of the strangest and worst jobs in science?—Jason Daley, freelance writer and editor, "The Worst Jobs in Science," *Popular Science*, February 2009; Jason Daley, freelance writer and editor, "The 10 Worst Jobs in Science," *Popular Science*, April 2010.

The happiest job in science?—Jason Daley, freelance writer and editor, "The 10 Worst Jobs in Science," *Popular Science*, April 2010; Hara Estroff Marano, editor-at-large, "The Benefits of Laughter," *Psychology Today*, February 25, 2010.

Russia's top space researchers are very worried about 99942 Apophis, an asteroid that will pass relatively near Earth starting in 2029. What do they want to do about it, and why do most American

scientists think that's a waste of time?—Ellen Barry, foreign correspondent, "Russia to Plan Deflection of Asteroid from Earth," *New York Times*, December 30, 2009.

Did you hear the one about the robot and the volleyball? Or is it the robotic volleyball?—Alex Hutchinson, contributing editor, "Gooey Robots Slip Through the Cracks," *Popular Mechanics*, February 2010.

What surprising bit of news did the world learn about Neanderthals in 2010?—Stephen S. Hall, science writer, "Last of the Neanderthals," *National Geographic*, October 2008; João Zilhão, archaeologist, Bristol University, England, et al., "Symbolic Use of Marine Shells and Mineral Pigments By Iberian Neanderthals," *Proceedings of the National Academy of Sciences*, January 11, 2010.

What's the oldest thing on Earth, and what has it taught us?—Kenneth Chang, science reporter, "Ancient Bit of Rock May Alter Theories of Earth's History," *New York Times*, January 11, 2001; Kenneth Chang, "A New Picture of the Early Earth," *New York Times*, December 2, 2008.

What's about the worst thing that can happen to Earth?—Christopher Mims, science and environment writer, "What Is the Worst Possible Disaster that Could Befall Earth?" *Popular Science*, February 2009.

What would happen to Earth if the sun went away?—Holly Otterbein, writer/editor, "If the Sun Went Out, How Long Would Life on Earth Survive?" *Popular Science*, November 2008.

What's the biggest science experiment ever?—"The Biggest Science Experiment Ever," *Popular Science*, December 2008; Hannah Devlin, science reporter, "Large Hadron Collider Switched on After Year of Repairs," *London Times*, October 28, 2009; Paddy Power, PLC, a betting and bookmaking firm based in Dublin.

What's the most ambitious engineering project ever?—"A Tunnel Through the Alps," *Popular Science*, March 2009.

Is it possible for a car to travel 1,000 mph?—Bloodhound Project; TheSuperCars.org.

What's 1,000 miles northeast of Hawaii, doubles in size every ten years and is about twice the size of Texas?—Lindsey Hoshaw, freelance journalist, "Afloat in the Ocean, Expanding Islands of Trash," *New York Times*, November 10, 2009.

How much water do Americans flush down the toilet every second, and why is that a waste—in more ways than one?—Josh Harkinson, staff reporter, "Trickle-down Theory," *Mother Jones*, July–August, 2009.

How many gallons of water are used to make a diaper, a cotton T-shirt, a ream of white paper, and a pair of leather shoes?—Jen Phillips, assistant editor, "Big Gulp," *Mother Jones*, July–August, 2009; Golf Course Superintendents Association of America.

E. coli has a pretty lousy reputation. Is it good for anything?—Corey Binns, science writer, "The Gas Bug," *Popular Science*, November 2008.

Next thing you're going to say is that you can make biodiesel from chicken feathers?—Henry Fountain, science reporter, "Diesel, Made Simply from Coffee Grounds (Ah, the Exhaust Aroma)," *New York Times*, December 16, 2008; "Oil in Your Coffee," *Economist*, February 4, 2009; Narasimharao Kondamudi, researcher, University of Nevada–Reno, et al., "Green Process for Producing Biodiesel from Feather Meal," *Journal of Agricultural and Food Chemistry*, June 25, 2009.

Where is the world's most energy-efficient skyscraper?—Jonathan Cheng, reporter, "Big Chinese Companies Take to the Sky," *Wall Street Journal*, January 13, 2010.

For more than a century, psychologists have offered the world a host of psychological explanations for our dreams: They allow us to act out our primal wants. They highlight our fears. They help us work through our problems. What if all that is a bunch of hooey?—J. Allan Hobson, professor of psychiatry emeritus, Harvard University, "REM Sleep and Dreaming: Towards a Theory of Protoconsciousness," *Nature Reviews Neuroscience*, November 2009.

6

The Berlin Wall came down in 1989, but what creature still refuses to cross the border?—Cecilie Rohwedder, reporter, "Deep in the Forest, Bambi Remains the Cold War's Last Prisoner," *Wall Street Journal*, November 4, 2009; "One Wall Was More Than Enough," *Newsweek*, November 16, 2009.

By far the best-preserved woolly mammoth ever found, in May 2007 in northwestern Siberia, was promptly stolen and sold to an unsuspecting shop owner. What did the thieves get for it?—Tom Mueller, writer, "Ice Baby," *National Geographic*, May 2009.

When is a male fish also a female fish?—Eric Hagerman, freelance writer, "The Canary in the River," *Popular Science*, December 2009.

Duct tape, one of the most essential items in any toolbox, may have its dominance threatened thanks to what lizard?—Arianne Cohen, contributing writer, "A Sticky Little Lizard Inspires a New Adhesive Tape," *New York Times*, February 24, 2010.

With the nation's current fascination with vampires, which members of the animal kingdom, besides the obvious (female mosquitoes and vampire bats), suck blood?—Natalie Angier, reporter, "A Taste for Blood," *New York Times*, October 21, 2008.

Researchers have long known that pigs are pretty smart. They can herd sheep, open and close cages, follow other pigs that are on the trail of food, and deceive if it suits them. What recent discovery has further enhanced their reputation for being (relatively) smart?—Donald M. Broom, professor of animal welfare, University of Cambridge, et al., "Pigs Learn What a Mirror Image Represents and Use It to Obtain Information," *Animal Behaviour*, November 2009.

What's the relative R-value for the blubber that allows polar bears to survive the cold season?—Bill Streever, author, *Cold: Adventures in the World's Frozen Places*, (Little, Brown & Company, 2009); Lindsay Barnett, reporter, "Bizarre Baldness Strikes Female Spectacled Bears In Leipzig Zoo," *Los Angeles Times*, November 3, 2009.

Tiny, James Bond-like tracking devices are providing biologists with information that is changing the way they view insects, birds, fish, and other creatures. What are some of the more surprising things they've learned?—Murray Carpenter, writer, "Unraveling Nature's Social Networks," *Popular Science*, February 2010.

For years entomologists marveled at how efficiently ants carried away their dead brethren before pathogens could infect the community. Researchers thought they knew why, but they didn't. What did they learn?—Dong-Hwan Choe, graduate student, Department of Entomology, University of California–Riverside, et al., "Chemical Signals Associated with Life Inhibit Necrophoresis in Argentine Ants," *Proceedings of the National Academy of Sciences USA*, May 19, 2009; Daniel Kronauer, junior fellow in Harvard's Society of Fellows, et al., "Colony Fusion and Worker Reproduction After Queen Loss in Army Ants," *Proceedings of the Royal Society B*, November 4, 2009.

Charlotte's Web aside, entomologists know spiders as vicious predators. Are there any kinder and gentler types?—Christopher J. Meehan, entomologist, University of Arizona, et al., "Herbivory in a Spider Through Exploitation of an Ant–plant Mutualism," *Current Biology*, October 2009.

What's the strongest animal in the world?—Smithsonian National Zoological Park website.

The Alaskan Upis beetle freezes at about minus 19 degrees F but can survive at minus 100 degrees F. How is that possible?—Kent R. Walters Jr., researcher, University of Notre Dame, et al., "A Nonprotein Thermal Hysteresis-Producing Xylomannan Antifreeze in the Freeze-Tolerant Alaskan Beetle *Upis ceramboides*," *Proceedings of the National Academy of Sciences of the United States of America*, November 23, 2009.

Alaskan Upis beetles are hardcore, but what's the toughest, most resilient creature on Earth?—Corey Binns, science writer, "Bears in Space," *Popular Science*, December 2008.

What single-cell creature communicates in two languages, loves company, identifies friend from foe, and spreads misinformation?—Lee R. Swem, molecular biologist, Princeton University, et al., "A Quorum-Sensing Antagonist Targets Both Membrane-Bound and Cytoplasmic Receptors and Controls Bacterial Pathogenicity," *Molecular Cell*, July 31, 2009.

How long can tarantulas live without food?—National Geographic Society.

Most people know blue whales are the world's largest mammals, but what's the smallest mammal?—Smithsonian National Zoological Park website.

Are there any places in the world where snakes don't live in the wild?—Smithsonian National Zoological Park website.

Rats have such a bad reputation as plague starters, among other things, so why are they given hero status in the African nations of Tanzania and Mozambique?—Alan Mairson, freelance journalist, "Ratted Out," *National Geographic*, October 2008.

After the fiddler crab leaves its home to forage for food, how does it find its way back?—Michael L. Walls, researcher, and John E. Layne, assistant professor, biological sciences, University of Cincinnati, "Direct Evidence for Distance Measurement via Flexible Stride Integration in the Fiddler Crab," *Current Biology*, December 24, 2008.

The star-nosed mole—arguably the most bizarre-looking creature on Earth, with incredibly long, white, fingernail-like claws, a hairy body, and a pink snout that resembles two sea stars stuck together—is also virtually blind, but what incredibly important distinction does it hold?—Jennifer S. Holland, senior writer, "Fleet Eater," *National Geographic*, October 2009.

Termites, though feared, mostly live in obscurity, munching away at your tree stump or your garage or your house, but when they're not working, what do they do in their spare time?—Lisa Margonelli, writer, "Gut Reactions," *Atlantic*, September 2008.

Argentine ants have been called one of the world's most destructive pests, wiping out crops and other ant species and invading homes. The extraordinarily tiny ants have traveled from their native Argentina to every continent except Antarctica. How have they become so dominant?—Tom

O'Neill, staff writer, "Ants on the March," *National Geographic*, December 2009.

Arguably the nastiest of insects, wasps have earned their reputation, but do they have a heart?—Sylvain-Jacques Desjardins, international press attaché, University of Montreal, "Ladybugs Taken Hostage by Wasps," *Nouvelles*, November 17, 2009.

Scientists thought they pretty much had bees figured out, but they recently learned bees have something in common with people. What?—Aurore Avarguès-Weber, PhD student, Université de Toulouse, et al., "Configural Processing Enables Discrimination and Categorization of Face-Like Stimuli in Honeybees," *Journal of Experimental Biology*, January 29, 2010; Megan Rauscher, reporter, "Can't Recognize Faces? It May Be Prosopagnosia," *Reuters Health*, June 9, 2006.

What creature can grow to fifty feet long and twenty-two tons and has 90,000 brethren but is rarely seen?—Jennifer S. Holland, senior writer, "In Hot Pursuit," *National Geographic*, October 2009.

Northern elephant seals are renowned for their Pacific Ocean swims, which can last two to eight months at a time, with 90 percent of that time on deep-sea dives. When do they sleep?—Yoko Mitani, a marine biologist affiliated with National Institute of Polar Research in Tokyo, Hokkaido University and Texas A&M University, et al., "Three-Dimensional Resting Behaviour of Northern Elephant Seals: Drifting Like a Falling Leaf," *Biology Letters*, October 28, 2009.

Guide dogs for the blind are by far the most popular "service animals" recognized by the Americans with Disabilities Act. What are some of the rarest ones?—Rebecca Skloot, freelance science writer, "Creature Comforts," *New York Times Magazine*, January 4, 2009; Civil Rights Division, U.S. Department of Justice.

When did wild cats become house cats?—Carlos Driscoll, a member of the University of Oxford's Wildlife Conservation Research Unit, et al., "The Taming of the Cat," *Scientific American*, June 2009.

Captive tigers have killed at least fifty-two people and injured hundreds in the past decade, so how has that curbed their appeal as pets?—Ronald Tilson and Philip Nyhus, authors, *Tigers of the World*, 2nd ed. (Elsevier, 2010); eHow.com.

There are only two egg-laying mammals left in the world. What are they, and what does new research say about how they survived when others did not?—Matthew J. Phillips, evolutionary biologist, Australian National University, et al.,"Molecules, Morphology, and Ecology Indicate a Recent, Amphibious Ancestry for Echidnas," *Proceedings of the National Academy of Sciences USA*, September 23, 2009.

What do scientists know about toucans' beaks besides the fact that they're really, really long?—Glenn J. Tattersall, biologist, Brock University, Ontario, et al., "Heat Exchange from the Toucan Bill Reveals a Controllable Vascular Thermal Radiator," *Science*, July 24, 2009.

Llamas are high-maintenance creatures that won't think twice about spitting on someone who annoys them, but how might they someday make an enormous impact on mankind?—Matthew Dalton, reporter, "When a Llama Is Laid Back, It's Not the Only Beneficiary," *Wall Street Journal*, February 17, 2009.

Humans have discovered 1.8 million or so living species since we started keeping track in 1758. Is this job about wrapping up by now?—International Institute for Species Exploration at Arizona State University, et al., "2009 State of Observed Species"; Wildlife Conservation Society.

Charles Darwin observed it when he visited the Galapagos Islands: Animals there are less aggressive and less afraid. Why?—Olivia Judson, evolutionary biologist, "Fearless," *New York Times*, February 2, 2010.

7

Is it true that underdogs have more motivation because they have a chip on their shoulders and want to knock off the favored teams?—Robert Lount, assistant professor, Ohio State University, et al., "Looking Down and Ramping Up: The Impact of Status Differences on Effort in Intergroup Contexts," *Journal of Experimental Social Psychology*, January 2010.

"Miracle on Ice," the stunning 4–3 victory by the young amateur U.S. hockey team over the veteran professional Soviet team in the 1980 Winter Olympics, is one of the greatest upsets in sports history and has been the subject of numerous books, but what don't most people know about the event?—Joe Pasnanski, senior writer, "10 Interesting Facts You May Not Know About the Miracle on Ice," *SportsIllustrated.cnn.com*, February 22, 2010.

Winter Olympians obviously train for years to get a chance to compete for precious medals, but how much time do medal winners actually spend performing their events?—Adam Thompson, staff reporter, "How a Few Seconds of Work Can Earn You Gold," *Wall Street Journal*, February 16, 2010; Christa Case Bryant, Middle East editor, "Weathering the Olympics: How Science and Sport Meet on the Bottom of a Ski," *Christian Science Monitor*, February 16, 2010.

How preposterous is it to say that the best National Football League quarterbacks are the best-looking quarterbacks?—Kevin M. Williams, senior research associate, Multi-Health Systems, Inc., Toronto, et al., "The Face Reveals Athletic Flair: Better National Football League Quarterbacks Are Better Looking," *Personality and Individual Differences*, January 2010.

Who was the most loyal sports fan?—Jim Carlton, reporter, "Gridiron Grind: This Poor Fan Never Misses a Kansas State Game," *Wall Street Journal*, November 14–15, 2009.

If you're a soccer goaltender trying to stop a penalty kick, which way should you dive—left or right?—Michael Bar Eli, professor, Ben-Gurion University of the Negev, "Action Bias Among Elite Soccer Goalkeepers: The Case of Penalty Kicks," *Journal of Economic Psychology*, February 9, 2008.

Which country loves soccer the most—the soccer powers of England, Italy, Germany, or Brazil?—

Simon Kuper, sports columnist, and Stefan Szymanski, economist, *Soccernomics: Why England Loses, Why Germany and Brazil Win, and Why the U.S., Japan, Australia, Turkey—and Even Iraq—Are Destined to Become the Kings of the World's Most Popular Sport* (Nation Books, 2009).

In 2010, Minnesota Twins all-star catcher Joe Mauer signed an eight-year, $184-million contract that will pay him $63,000 a day. What perk does he receive thanks to the league's collective bargaining agreement?—Major League Baseball.

Which Major League Baseball team keeps its baseballs in a humidor—and why?—Stuart Fox, writer, "Why Do the Colorado Rockies Keep their Baseballs in a Humidor?" *Popular Science*, November 2008.

Denver isn't the only place where baseballs are pampered, right?—Jeremy Berlin, editor, "The Dirt on Baseball," *National Geographic*, October 2008; eHow.com.

The average marathon race times have increased from about three and a half hours for men and four hours for women in 1980 to about four and a quarter hours for men and four and three-quarter hours for women today. Is this because we're becoming fatter and slower?—MarathonGuide.com.

When Major League Baseball teams spend oodles of money to attract star players, how many more games do they win on average the first season these players suit up for them?—David Biderman, sports reporter, "Additional Payroll Often Produces Fewer Wins," *Wall Street Journal*, November 17, 2009; Harvard Sports Analysis Collective.

In which North American professional sports league does money spent and wins correlate more often than not?—David Biderman, sports reporter, "In the NHL, More Dollars Equals More Wins," *Wall Street Journal*, December 14, 2009.

At what age do National Basketball Association players peak?—David Biderman, sports reporter, "After Age 25, It's All Downhill for NBA Players," *Wall Street Journal*, December 23, 2009.

What percentage of men say they wouldn't date a woman who doesn't follow football well enough to know who's playing in the Super Bowl?—match.com, an Internet dating service; "Book of Odds," an online reference that provides odds on everyday life; Nielsen.

The National Football League Pro Bowl is the only major league all-star game played at the end of the season, and players who are nursing injuries—either real or imagined—often skip it while those who participate often don't play hard and risk injury. How much money do they make to play in the game?—Reed Albergotti, staff reporter, "Making the Pro Bowl Doesn't Always Pay," *Wall Street Journal*, January 30–31, 2010.

8

Which has been the most politically corrupt state in recent years?—U.S. Census Bureau; U.S. Department of Justice; Bill Marsh, Week in Review graphics editor, "Illinois Is Trying. It Really Is. But the Most Corrupt State Is Actually . . ." *New York Times*, December 14, 2008.

The least corrupt state?—U.S. Census Bureau; U.S. Department of Justice; *State Politics and Policy Quarterly*; Bill Marsh, Week in Review graphics editor, "Illinois Is Trying. It Really Is. But the Most Corrupt State Is Actually . . ." *New York Times*, December 14, 2008.

The vast majority of Secret Service agents, especially the ones who guard presidents, are a tight-lipped bunch. Have any spilled the beans with anything juicy?—Eve Conant, reporter, "Can the Secret Service Keep a Secret," *Newsweek*, December 21, 2009.

Speaking of President Obama, his worst nightmare came true in 2010, when Republican Scott Brown became a U.S. senator, depriving Senate Democrats—and Obama—of the sixtieth vote they needed to pass legislation without Republican support. Brown's victory immediately led to the overhaul of Obama's ambitious initiative to pass a national health care bill. What do Obama and Brown

have in common?—"Kin If Not Allies: Obama, New Senator Are Related," *Associated Press*, January 30, 2010.

The health care bill of 2009 has been called one of the most voluminous pieces of legislation in American history—as well as some other much less complimentary things. How big was it?—Janet Adamy, reporter, "Does This Bill Have a Weight Problem?" *Wall Street Journal*, November 7–8, 2009; Congressional Budget Office.

Of our last twelve presidents, whose approval rating rose and plummeted the most in his first year in office?—"Opening Acts," *Atlantic*, January/February 2010; Office of Management and Budget.

American presidents have also gotten bad press for pardoning exiled scoundrels and other well-connected crooks, but what's up with South Korea's President Lee Myung-bak?—Embassy of the Republic of Korea; "Pardon Me," *Economist*, August 14, 2008.

Which country has the best voter turnout and which has the worst?—International Foundation for Electoral Systems; International Institute for Democracy and Electoral Assistance; Shelley Sperry, freelance writer, "Electoral Collage," *National Geographic*, November 2008.

What's the most anyone has paid (per vote) to win an election?—Michael Barbaro, reporter, "With Late Rush, Mayor Spent $102 Million on Election," *New York Times*, November 28, 2009; "Bloomberg's Spending Hits $102 Million for Campaign," *Associated Press*, November 27, 2009; "What's Your Vote Worth?" *Newsweek*, November 16, 2009.

President Barack Obama, who vowed to take the politics out of government, attended how many fund-raisers for the Democratic Party and its candidates during his first year as president?—Harper's Index, *Harper's*, January 2010.

President Richard Nixon was fond of making declarations, such as when he said the United States should cure cancer by 1976. What other declaration was way off the mark?—U.S. Department of Energy.

Not to pile on Nixon, but when it comes to presidents taking responsibility for blunders, he isn't exactly a paragon. How long did it take him to apologize for Watergate?—Andrew Romano, senior writer, "Sorry About That?" *Newsweek*, January 18, 2010; Tom O'Leary, blogger, "5 Steps to an Effective Apology," PickTheBrain.com, August 20, 2007.

As governor of Texas and as president, George W. Bush railed against frivolous lawsuits, so what's this about Bush suing a rental car company over a fender-bender?—Timothy Burger, reporter, "Bush Sued Enterprise Rent-A-Car Over Daughter's Fender Bender," *New York Daily News*, August 26, 2000; "Bush Signed Texas Bill Curbing Lawsuits but Filed One Himself," *Los Angeles Times*, August 27, 2000.

Climate change has become a front-burner environmental—and political—issue. Proof of the political part is the number of lobbyists knocking on congressmen's doors in Washington. How many are there?—Rachel Morris, articles editor, "Agents of Climate Change," *Mother Jones*, November/December 2009; Center for Public Integrity.

Most people would guess—and they'd guess right—that Nevada has the highest divorce rate in the United States. Which has the lowest?—U.S. National Center for Health Statistics; the Census Bureau's 2009 Statistical Abstract of the United States; Laura Vanderkam, writer, "When the Honeymoon Is Over," *Wall Street Journal*, March 6–7, 2010.

Republican candidates—at least at the federal level—have talked up conservative family values more than Democrats. Is there anything to that?—U.S. Census Bureau's 2009 Statistical Abstract; The Guttmacher Institute; Charles M. Blow, visual columnist, "The Prurient Trap," *New York Times*, June 27, 2009.

What percentage of Americans favors allowing "homosexuals" to serve in the military, and what percentage allows "gay men and lesbians" to serve?—CBS News/*New York Times* poll.

Is it true that husbands and wives who spend more time scrubbing the floors and doing the laundry together carve out less time to snuggle in the bedroom?—Constance T. Gager, assistant professor of family and child studies, Montclair State University, and Scott T. Yabiku, associate professor of sociology, Arizona State University, "Who Has the Time? The Relationship Between Household Labor Time and Sexual Frequency," *Journal of Family Issues*, October 9, 2009.

What percentage of marriages survive infidelity?—Sue Shellenbarger, work and family columnist, "Work & Family Mailbox," *Wall Street Journal*, March 31, 2010; Michael J. Glantz, neuro-oncologist, University of Utah School of Medicine, et al., "Gender Disparity in the Rate of Partner Abandonment in Patients with Serious Medical Illness," *Cancer*, November 15, 2009.

What percentage of Americans said they would act immorally to keep their jobs?—Adecco North America, a job placement firm.

What percentage of American males ages eighteen to twenty-nine believe that standing up during sex will prevent pregnancy?—National Campaign to Prevent Teen and Unplanned Pregnancy.

What percentage of English women say they've never—not once—had sex while sober?—"Sobering Thought," OnePoll, a global market research firm, September 23, 2009.

What's the most promiscuous bird in the world?—Chris S. Elphick, assistant professor of ecology and evolutionary biology, University of Connecticut, et al., "Extreme Levels of Multiple Mating Characterize the Mating System of the Saltmarsh Sparrow," *Auk*, April 2010.

Fellatio has been thought to be the sole domain of humans and bonobo chimpanzees, but, no, scientists recently discovered another species likes to do it, and it practices its own unique technique. What, er, who is it?—Tom Chivers, reporter, "Fellatio Common Among Fruit Bats, Says Research," *London Telegraph*, November 10, 2009.

Most male bedbugs that want to have sex are not the least bit particular about their partners—male, female, they don't care. What have researchers discovered about male bedbugs that aren't in the

mood to have sex with other males?—Camilla Ryne, chemical ecologist, Lund University, Sweden, et al., "Homosexual Interactions in Bed Bugs: Alarm Pheromones as Male Recognition Signals," *Animal Behaviour*, December 2009.

In Chicago, what's more likely to happen: that a prostitute will have sex for free with a police officer or that a police officer will arrest her for prostitution?—Steven D. Levitt and Sudhir A. Venkatesh, economists, "An Empirical Analysis of Street-Level Prostitution," a working paper, September 2007.

9

King Tut is arguably the world's best-known mummy because his remains have been studied so extensively, but what did scientists only recently discover about him?—Zahi Hawass, an Egyptologist who leads the Supreme Council of Antiquities, in Cairo, et al., "Ancestry and Pathology in King Tutankhamun's Family," *Journal of the American Medical Association*, February 17, 2010.

Why are archaeologists so excited about the 200 or so inhabitants of a 4,000-year-old cemetery in a Chinese desert just north of Tibet?—Nicholas Wade, science reporter, "A Host of Mummies, A Forest of Secrets," *New York Times*, March 15, 2010.

Much is known about Adolf Hitler because much has been written about him, but what are some things that only Hitler scholars may know?—Thomas Vinciguerra, freelance writer, "Dinner with the Führer," *New York Times*, March 8, 2009.

Speaking of dictators, Saddam Hussein moved constantly from palace to palace in Iraq for security reasons, but what security measure surprised his debriefers the most?—National Security Archive, a private research group at George Washington University.

Conspiracy theorists who believe Lee Harvey Oswald did not act alone when he killed President John F. Kennedy often point to a 1963 photo of Oswald holding a rifle that they say has obviously been doctored. True?—Alex Hutchinson, contributing editor, "Solo Act," *Popular Mechanics*, March 2010.

The USS *Monitor*, the famous Civil War ironclad that sunk off the coast of North Carolina during a storm in the wee hours of December 31, 1862, is well-known for its fight to a draw with the Confederate ironclad, the *Virginia*. When its turret was raised about 145 years later, what was one of the oddest discoveries onboard?—Chuck Myers, reporter, McClatchy-Tribune News Service, "USS Monitor Center is an Ironclad Adventure," *San Diego Union-Tribune*, April 8, 2007; Rich Asaro, docent, The Mariners' Museum, Newport News, Virginia.

The United States has held elections on the first Tuesday after the first Monday in November for nearly 170 years. Why Tuesday? Why November? And why not the first Tuesday?—Robert Longley, U.S. government guide, About.com.

What didn't you learn about our founding fathers in school that would have made American history class a lot more interesting?—Terry L. Jordan, *The U.S. Constitution and the Fascinating Facts About It* (Oak Hill Publishing Company, 2008); National Museum of Dentistry; Ioan James, *Asperger's Syndrome and High Achievement* (Jessica Kingsley Publishers, 2006).

Which presidents gave the shortest and longest inauguration speeches?—Terry L. Jordan, writer, *The U.S. Constitution and the Fascinating Facts About It* (Oak Hill Publishing Company, 2008); *Harrison's Inauguration: American Treasures of the Library of Congress*; Bartleby. com; James D. Richardson, *A Compilation of the Messages of the Presidents 1789–1897*, vol. 1.

Is there any link between President Lincoln and the Secret Service?—U.S. Secret Service.

What don't most Americans know about the Constitution?—Terry L. Jordan, writer, *The U.S. Constitution and the Fascinating Facts About It* (Oak Hill Publishing Company, 2008).

10

On a scale of one to ten, with one being not annoyed and ten being "annoys you tremendously," what bugs Americans the most?—"Top Gripes: What Bugs America Most," *Consumer Reports*, January 2010.

Which nation's workers get the most vacation time?—Mercer Consulting; Evan Ramstad and Jaeyeon Woo, reporters, "South Korea Works Overtime to Tackle Vacation Shortage," *Wall Street Journal*, March 1, 2010; numerous human resources professionals.

What percentage of American workers are satisfied with their jobs, and what are some companies doing about it?—Sue Shellenbarger, work and family columnist, "Thinking Happy Thoughts at Work," *Wall Street Journal*, January 27, 2010; Max Colchester, news assistant, "Managers' Bonuses Will Be Tied to Morale," *Wall Street Journal*, March 26, 2010.

What's the most common computer password, and if you use it, why should you change it?—Ashlee Vance, reporter, "If Your Password is 123456, Just Make It HackMe," *New York Times*, January 20, 2010; Michael Moyer, "The Everything TV," staff editor and writer, *Scientific American*, November 2009.

When it comes to passing along malware, which countries' domains are the most and least dangerous?—*The 2009 Mapping the Mal Web Report*, McAfee, Inc., December 2, 2009.

Which country's hackers most worry the IT executives charged with protecting their companies from cyberattacks?—Stewart Baker, visiting fellow, "In the Crossfire: Critical Infrastructure in the Age of Cyberwar," Center for Strategic and International Studies, September 2009.

Does anyone really read spam e-mail?—Chris Kanich, graduate student, University of California, San Diego, et al., "Spamalytics: An Empirical Analysis of Spam Marketing Conversion," *Communications of the ACM*, September 2009.

Does the background color of your computer screen help you compute or write better?—Ravi Mehta, PhD student, and Rui (Juliet) Zhu, assistant professor of marketing, University of British Columbia, "Blue or Red? Exploring the Effect of Color on Cognitive Task Performances," *Science*, February 5, 2009.

The average home buyer sees ten to twelve properties before deciding on a house. What's the most anyone has seen before buying?—Juliet Chung, reporter, "A Picky Home Buyer Pursues

An Epic Hunt for 'the One,' " *Wall Street Journal*, December 29, 2009; numerous real estate agents.

Which are the happiest and saddest states in the nation?—Andrew J. Oswald, economics professor, University of Warwick, in England, and Stephen Wu, economics professor, Hamilton College, in Clinton, N.Y., "Objective Confirmation of Subjective Measures of Human Well-Being: Evidence from the U.S.A.," *Science*, December 17, 2009.

Who are the worst drivers—teenage boys or girls?—Allstate Foundation; General Motors Acceptance Corporation (GMAC) Insurance National Drivers Test; Julie Wernau, reporter, "Teen Drivers: Risk Gap Shrinks," *Tribune Newspapers*, February 20, 2010.

If you're a lousy driver, can you blame it on your parents?—Steven C. Cramer, associate professor of neurology, University of California–Irvine, and Jeffrey A. Kleim, associate professor of neuroscience, University of Florida, et al., "BDNF Val[66]Met Polymorphism Influences Motor System Function in the Human Brain," *Cerebral Cortex*, September 10, 2009.

Where do the fastest and slowest highway drivers live?—TomTom, an Amsterdam-based company that sells digital mapping products.

What was the worst car ever built, and why does it deserve that distinction?—Dick Teresi, reviewer, "The Little Car That Couldn't," *Wall Street Journal*, March 4, 2010; Jason Vuic, author, *The Yugo* (Hill & Wang, 2010).

Is the sixty-four pack of Crayola crayons going to sixty-five?—Mas Subramanian, professor of material sciences, Oregon State University, et al., "Mn^{3+} in Trigonal Bipyramidal Coordination: A New Blue Chromophore," *Journal of the American Chemical Society*, November 9, 2009.

The debate over the wisdom—and effects—of spanking probably will never end, but is it growing or declining in popularity?—National Center for Health Statistics; Centers for Disease Control and Prevention.

How much plastic wrap do Americans buy per year?—Elizabeth Gettelman, managing editor, "Aboxalypse Now," *Mother Jones*, November/December 2009.

Authorities are discovering more and more marijuana farms in national forests. Who's to blame?—Joel Millman, reporter, "Mexican Pot Gangs Infiltrate Indian Reservations in U.S.," *Wall Street Journal*, November 5, 2009.

What percentage of poker players use drugs and other substances to improve their play?—Kevin A. Clauson, associate professor of pharmacy, Nova Southeastern University, Fort Lauderdale, Florida, et al., "Use of Cognitive and Performance Enhancing Medications in an International Sample of Self-Identified Poker Players," June 1, 2010.

Is there anything to lucky charms?—Car Bialik, columnist, "The Power of Lucky Charms," *Wall Street Journal*, April 29, 2010.

Is there a country that cares about world records more than any other?—Marc Lacey, correspondent, "Biggest Meatball? Most Kisses? Mexico Finds Records Grand," *New York Times*, September 8, 2009.

Where would you end up if you dug a hole in your backyard and kept digging until you reached the other end of the world?—Tom O'Neill, staff writer, "Polar Opposites," *National Geographic*, June 2009.

North Korea, the world's most closed nation, hasn't released revealing information about its economy for fifty years and hasn't shared meaningful demographic data since 1993. What did we learn about North Korea in 2010?—North Korean Economy Watch, a website devoted to North Korea; Evan Ramstad, staff reporter, "Pyongyang Reports an Aging, Less Healthy Population," *Wall Street Journal*, February 22, 2010; B. R. Myers, professor, Dongseo University, South Korea, "North Korea on the Edge," *Wall Street Journal*, March 27–28, 2010.

How many languages are spoken in the world today, and which are the most endangered?—A. R. Williams, writer, "A World Loses Its Tongues," *National Geographic*, October 2007;

Melody Kramer, freelance writer, "Who's Number Two?" *National Geographic*, September 2009; Nancy C. Rhodes, director and coauthor, and Ingrid Pufahl, project coordinator, "Foreign Language Teaching in U.S. Schools," Center for Applied Linguistics, November 2009; Jeremy Page, South Asia correspondent, "Last of the Bo Takes Her Language to the Grave As 65,000-Year-Old Tribe Dies Out," *London Times*, February 5, 2010.

Where on Earth was the Garden of Eden?—Sarah A. Tishkoff, associate professor of genetics and biology, University of Pennsylvania, et al., "The Genetic Structure and History of Africans and African Americans," *Science*, April 30, 2009; Genesis 2:8–14, New International Version Study Bible.

The Hadzas, a tribe in northern Tanzania, fascinates anthropologists. Why?—Michael Finkel, writer, "The Hadza," *National Geographic*, December 2009.

What percentage of Africans lives without electricity?—Cate Doty, news assistant, "For Africa, Energy from Dirt," *New York Times*, November 11, 2008.

Which countries by percentage have the smallest number of people with access to improved water sources?—2008 World Population Data Sheet; U.S. Department of Energy; Ellen Byron, staff reporter, "The Great American Soap Overdose," *Wall Street Journal*, January 27, 2010.

How far do women in developing nations walk on average per day to fetch water for their families?—Water Advocates; Federal Emergency Management Agency; Mark Jenkins, contributing writer, "High Marks For Clean Water," *National Geographic*, April 2010.

The collapse of the Soviet Union in 1991 was seen as a liberating experience for its people, but was Russia better off as a Communist nation?—World Health Organization, United Nations Educational Scientific and Cultural Organization, and the National Statistical Office of the Russian Federation.

Which countries are growing the fastest, and which are losing their population the fastest?—2008 World Population Data Sheet.

Which countries live in the most and least crowded conditions?—2008 World Population Data Sheet.

Which U.S. state retains most of its adults, and which retains the fewest?—Pew Research Center; U.S. Census Bureau.

Which state attracts the most adults, and which attracts the fewest?—Pew Research Center; U.S. Census Bureau.

Three U.S. towns claim a population of one, but none of them was counted first in the 2010 Census. Which was?—U.S. Census Bureau.

So much attention is given to the tallest, longest, shortest, most popular, and most populated. Who's in second place (with #1 in parentheses)?—Melody Kramer, freelance writer, "Who's Number Two?" *National Geographic,* September 2009; "World's Tallest Building Opens and Is Renamed," *Wall Street Journal,* January 5, 2010.

Which age group watches more TV—fourteen to twenty-five, twenty-six to forty-two, or forty-three to sixty-one?—Deloitte Services LP, a company that does a lot of things, including consulting.

Who are the world's dumbest criminals?—"World's Costliest Scrap Metal?" *New York Times,* May 20, 2009.

Do boys with good grooming habits do better in school than boys who don't care about tousled hair and dirty fingernails?—Michael T. French, professor of health economics, University of Miami, et al., "Effects of Physical Attractiveness, Personality and Grooming on Academic Performance in High School," *Labour Economics,* August 2009.

Do Americans appreciate unexpected freebies as much as, say, Asians?—Ana Valenzuela, assistant professor of marketing, Baruch College, et al., "Pleasurable Surprises: A

Cross-Cultural Study of Consumer Responses to Unexpected Incentives," *Journal of Consumer Research*, July 15, 2009.

Paris is widely considered one of the world's most romantic cities, but what has stunk up that reputation?—Susana Ferreira, reporter, "In Paris, Behavior Brigade Battles to Make Oui-Oui a Non-Non," *Wall Street Journal*, September 1, 2009.

What's the world's biggest and most expensive cruise ship, and what does it have going for it?—Rory Nugent, writer, "Hope Floats," *Atlantic*, June 2009; Sarah Nassauer, reporter, "What It Takes to Keep a City Afloat," *Wall Street Journal*, March 3, 2010.

How long does it take to take the stairs to the observation deck of the Empire State Building?—Liz Robbins, sports writer, "Great Workout, Forget the View," *New York Times*, February 19, 2009.

When it comes to housing, New York City is known for its high-rise condos, brownstones, and tenement apartment buildings, but few people, even there, realize the city offers another housing option. What is it?—Mark Van de Walle, freelance writer, "Single-Wides in the City?" *New York Times Magazine*, March 15, 2009.

F. Scott Fitzgerald is known as much for his rollicking, excessive, highbrow lifestyle that characterized the Roaring Twenties as for his novels, including *The Great Gatsby*, *The Beautiful and Damned*, *This Side of Paradise*, and *Tender Is the Night*. In 1936, how much did he receive in book royalties?—Arthur Krystal, essayist, screenwriter and author, "Slow Fade," *New Yorker*, November 16, 2009.

Curious George, the mischievous and lovable monkey, escaped an elevator operator, farmer, cook, zookeepers, and firefighters, all of whom wanted a piece of him for various reasons. But how did his creators, Margret and H. A. Rey, top his frequent escapes?—Edward Rothstein, cultural critic, "Monkey Business in a World of Evil," *New York Times*, March 25, 2010.

How often do we blink per minute?—Jennifer S. Holland, senior writer, "On the Blink," *National Geographic*, December 2008.

If someone hits you on purpose, does it hurt more than if it were an accident?—Kurt Gray, graduate student, and Daniel M. Weger, psychology professor, Harvard University, "The Sting of Intentional Pain," *Psychological Science*, July 2008.

If you're dreaming of an exceptionally white Christmas, where do you have the best chance of making your dream a reality?—National Climatic Data Center; National Operational Hydrologic Remote Sensing Center.

Why is it so hard to keep a New Year's resolution?—Jonah Lehrer, author, "Blame It on the Brain," *Wall Street Journal*, December 26–27, 2009.

Children of older fathers are better off because their dads are wiser, wealthier, and more mature, right?—John J. McGrath, professor of psychiatry, Queensland Brain Institute in Brisbane, Australia, et al., "Advanced Paternal Age Is Associated with Impaired Neurocognitive Outcomes during Infancy and Childhood," the online journal *PLoS Medicine*, March 9, 2009.

Is your child better off with a very good teacher in a bad school or with a bad teacher in a very good school?—Malcolm Gladwell, staff writer, "Most Likely to Succeed," *New Yorker*, December 15, 2008.

What percentage of an American child's life is spent under a school roof?—Chester E. Finn Jr., president of the Thomas B. Fordham Institute, "The Case for Saturday School," *Wall Street Journal*, March 20–21, 2010; Kaiser Family Foundation, a nonprofit group that publishes research on broad policy issues; Alliance for Childhood, a nonprofit group in Maryland that focuses on early education.

When is the best time for recess: before or after lunch?—Tara Parker-Pope, health reporter/columnist, "Play, Then Eat: Shift May Bring Gains at School," *New York Times*, January 25, 2010; Romina M. Barros, assistant clinical professor, Albert Einstein College of Medicine, et al., "School Recess and Group Classroom Behavior," *Pediatrics*, January 2009.

Only about half of all college entrants graduate within six years, but that group must be well-prepared to make it in the real world, right?—Thomas Toch, codirector of Education Sector, a nonprofit think tank, "Tell the Truth About Colleges," *Atlantic*, July–August 2009; National Center for Education Statistics.

How many allegedly incompetent and abusive public school teachers in New York City are paid to do nothing?—Steven Brill, lawyer/writer, "The Rubber Room," *New Yorker*, August 31, 2009.

Do others really look better as we drink more alcohol?—Vincent Egan, forensic psychologist at the University of Leicester, England; Giray Cordan, psychologist, University of Exeter, England, "Barely Legal: Is Attraction and Estimated Age of Young Female Faces Disrupted by Alcohol Use, Makeup and the Sex of the Observer?" *British Journal of Psychology*, June 2009.

When it comes to detecting underarm odor, who's better: men or women?—Charles J. Wysocki, adjunct professor of animal biology, University of Pennsylvania, et al., "Cross-Adaptation of a Model Human Stress-Related Odour with Fragrance Chemicals and Ethyl Esters of Axillary Odorants: Gender-Specific Effects," *Flavour and Fragrance Journal*, April 7, 2009.

How many women are head coaches of high school varsity football teams in the United States?—"Female Chief Named to Lead Mohegan Tribe," *Associated Press*, March 5, 2010.

Which book of the Bible makes no mention of God and avoids any reference to praying and worshipping?—Bible, New International Version.

How many hotels does the massive Ritz-Carlton Hotel Company own?—Ritz-Carlton Hotel Company, LLC; Marriott International, Inc.

Why do construction-related accidents in New York City often occur on Fridays?—Larissa MacFarquhar, staff writer, "Busted: The Investigators Who Try to Keep City Employees Honest," *New Yorker*, February 1, 2010.

Thousands of products—some say more than 5,000—come from trees and their by-products. What are some of the more unusual ones?—Idaho Forest Products Commission; Wells Timberland Real Estate Investment Trust.

INDEX

investing $10,000, 48
Iran
    source of kidney transplants, 10
    death penalty, 42
    nuclear weapons, 42
Iraq
    death penalty, 42
Israel
    kidney transplant program, 10
    black market sales of kidneys,
        10

Japan
    infant mortality rates, 39
    employee theft, 55
Japanese macaques, 90
Jefferson, Thomas, 149–50
job satisfaction, 156
Johnson, Lyndon B., 132, 134

K2, a.k.a. Savage Mountain, 171
Kansas State, University of, 122
Kennedy, John F., 134, 137
Kennedy, Robert F., 152
kidneys
    shortage for transplants, 10
killer cows, 34
King George VI, 175
King Tutankhamun
    cause of death, 145
Kluge, Patricia, 64
Korean War, 179
KPMG, 156

languages
    endangered, 167
    most popular, 167
Large Hadron Collider, 93
last-word speeches, 33–34
Las Vegas casinos
    security measures, 53
    gambling losses, 53
Lebone Solutions, 168
Lee, Myung-Bak, 134
leeches, 90, 104
Levin, Carl, 136
Lewinsky, Monica, 137
Lincoln, Abraham, 151
Lipson, Robert, 122
live-or-die limits, 35
llamas, 114
lunch
    most expensive, 58
lucky charms, 165

Macklowe, Harry, 63
Madison, James, 149
Madoff, Bernard, 54
Malawi, 85
Malerba, Lynn, 180
marathons, 125
marijuana
    level of addiction compared with other drugs,
        12
    farms in national forests, 164
marriages and infidelity, 139
Marriott International, 181
Mauer, Joe, 123

238 INDEX

McCain, John, 138
McCarthy, Cormac, 50
Medical College Admission Test, 7
medical mistakes, 37
Men's Health, 79
Mexican drug gangs, 164
Mexico
    world records, 165
Michaels, Al, 120
Minnesota Twins, 123
"Miracle on Ice," 120
Mohegans, 180
Moore, Henry, 172
Motor Trend, 163
Mount Sinai School of Medicine, 7
MS *Oasis of the Sea*, 173
mucus, 90
multivitamins
    benefits of, 13
Museum of Egyptian Antiquities, 11

naps
    frequency based on race and employment
        status, 28
National Archives Building, 152
National Women's Football Association,
    180
Neanderthals, 92
neckties
    germs they carry, 5–6
Nevado-Reno, University of, 96
New England Historic Genealogical Society,
    133
New Year's resolutions, 177

New York Hospital Medical Center of Queens,
    6
Nixon, Richard M.
    cancer cure goal, 27
    Secret Service secret, 132
    approval ratings, 134
    oil dependency declaration, 136
North Korea
    size of workforce and military, 166
    demographic and poverty data, 166
North Korean Economy Watch, 166
northern elephant seals, 112
Notre Dame, 61
nuclear weapons, 42
Nucor Corporation, 48
nursing home costs, 9

Obama, Barack, 48, 133, 136, 138
obesity
    percentage of American children, 19
    proximity to fast-food restaurants,
        19
    most obese nations, 20
    most obese states, 20
    least obese state, 20
    dangers compared with smoking, 22
office gambling pools, 70–71
Ohio State University, 49
Oregon State University, 163
Oswald, Lee Harvey, 147
overweight
    effects of, 21
oxpecker, 104
oxytocin, 29

INDEX